Copy "A"

This Book
has been presented to the
CHURCH LIBRARY
of *First Wayne*
Street United
Methodist Church
by

Pat Hinkle

'03

PUTTING
FAITH
TO WORK

and

STRENGTHENING
THE SPIRITUAL LIFE

Putting Faith To Work

ROBERT J. McCRACKEN

Strengthening the Spiritual Life

NELS F. S. FERRÉ

GUIDEPOSTS ASSOCIATES INC.

Carmel, New York

Guideposts edition published by arrangement with
Harper & Row, Publishers, Inc.

PRINTED IN THE UNITED STATES OF AMERICA

How These Two Books Can Help You

If a person's faith is to be relevant in the modern day world, it needs two elements: inner strength and outer thrust. This combination is not easy to acquire—or maintain. An individual with a strong inner core of faith often is not able to apply it to his outside world involving family, job, social life and community activities. Likewise, people who can relate their religious convictions to their everyday life are often plagued by such inner onslaughts on their faith as nagging doubts, depression, abnormal fears.

To help seekers in their quest for a balanced faith, Guideposts is publishing two books in this one volume. *Putting Faith to Work* by Robert J. McCracken is a reasoned, articulate call to action by one of America's outstanding preachers. Dr. McCracken offers the individual a specific direction to go if he is to relate his faith to the problems of our day.

In *Strengthening the Spiritual Life,* author Nels F. S. Ferré is concerned with the creative use of the elements which undergird ones interior faith: prayer, worship and the Bible. The author avoids theory and writes out of personal experience, bringing practical help to anyone who has trouble working out a personal devotional program.

These two books offer rich spiritual food for the deep human needs of our day.

THE EDITORS

PUTTING
FAITH
TO WORK

Robert J. McCracken

GUIDEPOSTS ASSOCIATES INC.
Carmel, New York

Grateful acknowledgment is made to the following for special permission to reprint copyrighted material from the works indicated. A full list of sources for quoted passages appears on pages 165 ff.

The *New York Herald Tribune:* "High Flight" by John Gillespie Magee, Jr. (Feb. 8, 1942).

Harper & Brothers, New York: selections from G. A. Studdert-Kennedy, "High and Lifted Up" and "The Suffering God," published in *The Sorrows of God and Other Poems,* copyright 1924 by Harper & Brothers and 1952 by Emily Studdert-Kennedy.

The Macmillan Company, New York: selection from J. B. Phillips, *Letters to Young Churches,* copyright 1947, 1957 by The Macmillan Company.

Charles Scribner's Sons, New York: "Work" reprinted with the permission of Charles Scribner's Sons from *The Three Best Things, The Poems of Henry van Dyke,* copyright 1911 by Charles Scribner's Sons; renewal copyright 1939 by Tertius van Dyke.

Jonathan Cape Limited, London: "Leisure" from the *Collected Poems of W. H. Davies,* copyright by Mrs. H. M. Davies and Jonathan Cape, Ltd., 1949.

For
M. I. McC.

CONTENTS

STRENGTHENING THE SPIRITUAL LIFE

PREFACE

It has been frequently suggested that the most damaging criticisms directed against Christianity in our time are that it is incredible and irrelevant.

This book sets itself to exhibit the reasonableness of Christian Faith and to promote a better understanding of it by showing what is involved for the mind and the intelligence.

At the same time it seeks to keep the exposition close to the contemporary situation and, in particular, to work out the social implications of the Gospel. Its unifying principle is that personal religion must be matched by social concern. To relate the Gospel to the dominant social forces in economic and political life is the business of every Christian witness and advocate.

R. J. McC.

Part One
TOWARD A MATURE FAITH

I

How Difficult Not to Believe in God

Just after the conclusion of World War II, I was invited to the home of a friend to meet a missionary. Somewhat to my surprise, he talked not about South America, his field of labor, but about Europe and the impressions standing out in his memory after revisiting it: the havoc, far greater than he had conceived, wrought by mass bombing; the contrast between abundance here and austerity there; the struggle to recover economic stability and security; the startling decline of interest in every kind of institutional religion; and over against all this, a sermon he had heard in bomb-scarred Birmingham, which had for its title "How Difficult Not to Believe in God." What was said that evening has come back to my mind again and again. Europe emerging painfully and laboriously from the most terrible trouble it had ever known, a whole way of life, a pattern of culture and civilization in the balance; and a preacher undertaking to deal with the obstacles to skepticism and agnosticism, with the problems confronting the person who proposes to reject belief in God.

I wish I could have heard the sermon. If anything, it would be even more apposite now. For thoughtful people, pondering the significance of what is happening across the world—the revolutions, the balance of terror between East and West, the threat posed by the race in nuclear armaments—belief in God cannot be facile. Faith today, in Pascal's metaphor, is a wager placed against heavy odds. There must be few who, as they reflect on the appalling amount of evil, cruelty, and suffering to which humanity is subject, do not have to come to grips with the question: How are such things to be reconciled with the existence of a God who is all-wise, all-powerful, and all-loving?

3

But, as the Birmingham preacher doubtless pointed out, there is another side to all this. There is good in the world as well as evil, pleasure as well as pain, kindness as well as cruelty. The tendency is to concentrate on one aspect, on the evil rather than the good, on the pain rather than the pleasure, on the cruelty rather than the kindness. It is a tendency to be seen in novels and plays and in fields as far apart as art and theology. It is not a tendency peculiar to our generation but it is probably more pronounced today than it ever was, and being so pronounced it justifies one in saying: The evil in the world shakes faith in God; what about the good? Why talk only about the problem of evil? Why not the problem of good? What right have we to take the good for granted and seek only an explanation of the evil? Surely what we ought to seek is an explanation of the world as a whole. And if the good is more positive and fundamental than the evil, the existence of the good is surely what needs most to be explained. Whatever the person who rejects the Christian hypothesis has to say about the evil in the world, he is under obligation to offer some account of the good that is in it—the beauty and bounty of nature, the unselfishness, nobility, and heroism of which human nature is capable.

We all recognize the presence in the universe of two opposing qualities: good and evil. If we refuse to believe in God, goodness is a mystery. Where did it come from? How did spiritual life arise out of an unspiritual source like the jungle mode of existence described by scientists as the only existence that early man knew? How did souls come from the dust? To rule out belief in God does not solve all our problems; it leaves greater problems unsolved. It *is* hard to believe in God; some of us, however, find it harder still not to believe in Him. Negation presents us with bigger difficulties than faith. One thing has to be set over against another: beauty against ugliness, love against hate, truth against error, right against wrong. If there is no God what are we to make of the emergence of personality and of the achievements of great personalities? How are we to account for the beauty of a Beethoven sonata? Was

Jesus, to quote a phrase coined by Bertrand Russell, simply "the outcome of accidental collocations of atoms"? I find it harder to believe that than to believe in God the Father Almighty, Maker of heaven and earth.

I do not minimize the problem presented by the "giant agony of the world." An easy faith is a contradiction in terms, insulting alike to conscience, mind, and heart. Great faith has always had to do battle with great doubt. We possess it only as we fight for it and recapture it day by day. One can understand Hugh Walpole making a young man in one of his novels exclaim: "You know there can't be a God, Vanessa. In your heart you must know it. You are a wise woman. You read and think. Well, then, ask yourself. How can there be a God and life be as it is?" One can understand that, but it is only one aspect of the case. A correspondent wrote to J. B. Pratt: "I have never seen a high mountain or the ocean or any other vast and beautiful sight, without a strengthening of my belief in God. And it is also true that I have never seen a miserable child, a suffering, abused animal or a fallen woman without the same effect. There *must* be some One by whom all these creatures shall be avenged." One thing has to be set over against another: beauty against ugliness, love against hate, truth against error, right against wrong. In our best moments we do not doubt that the real forces in the world are spiritual, are beauty, love, truth, right; and in the face of them we find it hard not to believe in God.

Take the great world of nature. There is an interpretation of that world which makes faith in a good God desperately difficult. I am thinking of those for whom nature is "red in tooth and claw," cruel, relentless, indifferent to moral issues. I am thinking of those who see an incessant struggle for survival going on in nature, a struggle in which the race is to the swift and the battle to the strong, and whatever is weak goes to the wall. I am thinking of those who ask how they are to reconcile faith in the Father-God with animals which seem the incarnation of cruelty, equipped with claws and fangs and suckers, instruments of torture and destruction. For some, this is the source of their deepest doubts and perplexities. "I confess," wrote Bishop Charles Gore, "that the glint of pain in an animal's eye remains, if not a valid argument against belief in God's goodness, yet, as often as my mind dwells on it, a source of unrelieved discomfort."

No sensitive person will minimize the problem presented here for faith, but he should not overlook the other side of the case. To speak of nature as "red in tooth and claw" is to tell only one part of the story. If it is the part of the story that has gripped you, you owe it to yourself to walk through the woods, to climb the hills, to listen to the music of running water, to drink in the beauty of the blue sky and the green fields, to keep an open eye for the breath-taking loveliness of nature: the sun going down like a ball of fire over land and sea, the moon riding high in the heavens, with great banks of snow-white clouds for its background. Some of us have discovered what was so basic for Jesus, that God draws near to us in the world He has made. In the glory and splendor of land and sea, of mountain and valley, we have found a deep door into the Infinite. John Gillespie Magee, killed in action at the age of nineteen when serving with the Royal Canadian Air Force, some days before his death wrote:

> Oh, I have slipped the surly bonds of earth,
> And danced the skies on laughter-silvered wings;
> Sunward I've climbed and joined the tumbling mirth
> Of sun-split clouds—and done a hundred things
> You have not dreamed of—wheeled and soared and swung
> High in the sunlit silence. Hov'ring there,
> I've chased the shouting wind along and flung
> My eager craft through footless halls of air.
> Up, up the long delirious, burning blue
> I've topped the wind-swept heights with easy grace,
> Where never lark, or even eagle flew;
> And, while with silent, lifting mind I've trod
> The high untrespassed sanctity of space,
> Put out my hand, and touched the face of God.

There was a lad who found it difficult not to believe in God.

As with nature, so with human nature. There is a doctrine

of man which makes faith in God not only irrelevant but in-credible. It refuses to allow human nature any supernatural basis. It sees the life of man as motivated by the incessant drives of hunger, power and sex. It interprets man in terms of his biological necessities. He is a part of the physicochemical world, a portion of matter, composed of hydrogen, carbon, nitrogen, phosphorus, calcium, and other elements. He is an animal, an economic and political animal, able to satisfy his wants in community under social control. But the material element is the primary and basic element in him. On this view, as Joseph Wood Krutch, formerly of Columbia University, contended some years ago, life is merely a physiological proc-ess with no more than a physiological meaning. Well, that is one interpretation of the nature of man, and it goes without saying that its effect is to rule out God entirely.

There is, however, another interpretation. It is that man is more than a conglomeration of chemical compounds. To be sure, he is in nature and of it; he is a part of the physicochemi-cal world, and subject to its laws; he has a bodily organism sympathetic with natural forces and acting in accordance with them; *but* he is more than a piece of nature. There are nameless longings in him that will not be stifled. He is capable of living his life from a great depth of being. His reach ex-ceeds his grasp. As Sir Thomas Browne expressed it, there is a "part of divinity" within him. Or as the Bible words it, he is made in the image and likeness of God and cannot live by bread alone. "Know this earth is not my sphere," cried Brown-ing, "for I cannot so narrow me but that I still exceed it." "The Kingdom of God," Jesus went about saying, "is within you." How that sentiment echoes and re-echoes in the world's liter-ature—that man is a finite center of consciousness but able to long for and apprehend Infinity, and never really happy until he is at one with Infinity.

This is what Karl Barth calls man's "incurable Godsick-ness," and in justification of the phrase he can point to evi-dence of a commanding character. Religion is a universal human phenomenon. In every country and in every century men have felt after God if haply they might find Him. Belief in God is instinctive; its foundations are deep in the human soul; it is like the homing instinct in the bird. In one form or another—and alas, it repeatedly takes perverted forms—it is a necessity. It is not an optional interest, an extra which is a means of satisfaction to some, but which leaves others cold. Man is so made that the instinct in him to worship is inherent and ineradicable. One of the facts about human nature which cannot be challenged is that it must have something to believe in, to belong to, to give itself to with heart and soul and mind. This is everywhere the presupposition of the teaching of Jesus.

Years ago a story was in circulation about a Russian girl who took a civil service examination, and when it was over was fearful about passing. One question especially she kept worrying about: "What is the inscription on the Sarmian wall?" She had written what she thought it was—"Religion is the opiate of the people"—but to be quite certain she walked the seven miles from Leningrad to the Sarmian wall. There it was, exactly as she had set it down in the paper: "Religion is the opiate of the people." Falling on her knees she crossed herself and said, "Thank God." Yes, the religious instinct is inherent and ineradicable. It is difficult not to believe in God. During the war we became familiar with the saying "There are no atheists in foxholes." There were apparently no atheists on Eddie Rickenbacker's raft. Are there any atheists anywhere? In his celebrated essay on the subject, Francis Bacon asserted that "atheism is rather in the lip than in the heart of man." All the evidence goes to suggest that he was right. People may deny God with the top of their minds, but they believe Him at the bottom of their hearts.

You may question the assertion. Without flying in the face of the facts, one thing you cannot question. All men recognize some Ultimate. If it is not God it is a substitute for Him: the Almighty Dollar, the *Führer*, the *Duce*, the Nation, the Proletariat Class. The ideologies of our time have all the marks of religions. Communism for its adherents is essentially a faith, and as such demands the submission of the whole man. It witnesses to the aching emptiness of the human spirit when it has turned away from God.

Do you see what all this means for you? By the very constitution of your nature you are made for God. You can never be finally content with a reading of the facts which sees life as a physiological process with no more than a physiological meaning. You have aspirations after something transcending and outlasting the immediate necessities of instinctive life; you have a consciousness, repressed but insurgent, that you belong to another order of things; you dream of beauty, goodness, and truth.

> Your destiny, your being's heart and home
> Is with Infinitude and only there.

Though you may not always recognize that it is so, your heart and soul cry out for the living God. Nothing less than God will ever meet your need. A soul without God is an empty, aching, homesick soul. "O Lord," exclaimed Jeremiah, "I know that the way of man is not in himself." Have you made that discovery? So many who have not wonder why life does not yield real happiness or abiding peace. It is because they are out of touch with their native element. It is because they are out of touch with God, who is the source of their life. They forget what Augustine stated so memorably: "God is the only Reality, and we are real only insofar as we are in His order and He in us."

II

Isn't Religion Old Stuff?
Hasn't Science Outmoded It?

The question confronting Christians today is often stated thus: Granted that there may be some evidence that God exists, what difference does belief in Him make? Have we not moved beyond the traditional doctrines into a new era of scientific understanding, to a point where God is no longer necessary? What is a mature faith in a time when science is in the ascendancy?

At a university club luncheon a faculty wife said to the wife of a minister, "We have no religion. My husband is a scientist." As it happens, my work as a minister in Scotland, Canada, and New York has been done in close proximity to universities, and the attitude reflected in that statement is one with which I have become familiar. It is not an attitude confined to university circles. The impression is widespread that science has weakened the case for religion, that religion is fighting a losing battle against the scientific view of the world, that belief in evolution, to take a specific case, leaves no room for the old-time concept of God, and that it is hard to conceive any sort of God reconcilable with the findings of modern physics. The increasing control by science, not only of the physical environment but of the processes of the mind, has meant that for many persons religion makes less and less difference to practical living. It is incontestable that the most serious competitor of the Christian faith in the world today is salvation by science—this even though scientific inventions threaten civilization with catastrophe. People stay away from churches and synagogues for any number of reasons. One of them is the idea that science is always moving ahead while religion is anchored to the past, is obscurantist, is a strain on the intelligence.

It has to be acknowledged that a great deal of religion, much of it calling itself the Christian religion, is obscurantist and an affront to the intelligence. Hollywood has made a film of Sinclair Lewis' novel *Elmer Gantry*—the story, exaggerated to the point of caricature, of a Christian minister. People, viewing it, may justifiably say, "If that is religion I wash my hands of it." It is the story of an archhypocrite whose Christianity had no relation to reason and little to morality; had all the weaknesses of Pietism and none of the strengths. Allowing for the exaggeration and distortion, Lewis' novel exposes a type of religion never without some vogue among us— the religion of the closed mind, hidebound to tradition, fearful of new truth, irrational, intolerant, born in ignorance, swaddled in sentimentality. The only thing to do with it is to wash one's hands of it, for it is a perversion of all that religion is meant to be. But there is another type of religion, openminded, forward-looking, a religion that regards the mind as a sacred instrument, and the pursuit of truth as a sacred duty, and that builds its adherents up in a faith that knows no fear of truth because its innermost conviction is that God is Truth.

It must also be acknowledged that science has greatly affected religious beliefs—beliefs about the universe, about man, about miracles, about the Bible. To begin with, when modern science had its rise, religion was on the defensive, resisting the findings of geology, biology, astronomy; dealing harshly with Copernicus, Galileo, Darwin. But with the passage of time it accepted those findings and went about the task of reinterpreting the Bible in the light of them. The reinterpretation emphasizes that the main concern of the Bible is with religion and morality; it was not given to teach us science. Science is concerned with *how* the universe works, *how* life develops. The Bible is concerned with *why* there is a universe at all, *why* there is such a thing as life, particularly human life. The Bible's chief interest is not in explaining the processes of nature but in proclaiming that behind all that exists there is a Supreme Power on whom the whole universe, including man, depends. The first chapter of Genesis, for instance, invites us to contemplate the wonder of the created world, to believe that God is its Author, and that He has given man a status in the world different from that of any other created being.

There is nothing obscurantist about this, nothing that science has outmoded. The discouraging thing is that so many otherwise well-informed people think religion is still occupying the position today that it did when the Science-versus-Religion controversy was at its height during the last century, or when William Jennings Bryan, having solemnly stated that he was convinced that the whale swallowed Jonah, went on to add that if the Bible had said that Jonah had swallowed the whale he would have believed that too. There is always a deplorable time lag between advances in knowledge and the mental attitude of the man in the street. Even so, one would have supposed that by this time Christian teaching had received sufficient exposition for educated people, at least, to avoid the most elementary mistakes in their references to it, but this is not the case. As Professor Edmund Sinnott of Yale University remarks, "Many 'liberals' have not gone to church for so long that they have not kept up with what is going on there." The Christianity they criticize is all too often an infantile brand which any literate Christian would repudiate with even greater finality. If you have ever attempted to find out what the average nonchurchgoer thinks or knows about the Church's teaching, you must have been appalled at the incredible amount of junk and jargon lodged in the recesses of his mind—garbled notions about the Bible, the assumption in instance after instance that religious faith is necessarily credulous and superstitious. Talk about religion being old stuff! The trouble is that so many of its critics are themselves not up to date. They have not taken the pains to find out what honest religion is about or what it has to offer.

Something of the kind is true even of churchgoers. They lack knowledge of the most elementary truths of the Bible.

They are aware that a change has taken place in the Church's attitude toward the Bible, but they have not made any effort to grasp what the change is. For their grandparents, the Bible was a book of answers to life's problems, authoritative and divinely certified; for them, it is largely unknown and unexplored territory. They have moved on in their knowledge of other subjects—politics, economics, literature, music—but in their knowledge of Christianity they have stood still. Sometimes, ironically enough, you will hear them say, "The Church is behind the times, it is not progressive." In point of fact it is they who are behind the times, and in matters of faith if not actually infantile at least no more than juvenile. They read magazines and books in plenty, but few that have to do specifically with Christianity. As for the Bible, if they were frank, they would admit that with the exception of familiar passages in the Gospels, Epistles, and Psalms, they are at a loss to know what to make of it.

Something Dorothy L. Sayers wrote about Great Britain applies equally to this country:

It is hopeless to offer Christianity as a vaguely idealistic aspiration of a simple and consoling kind; it is, on the contrary, a hard, tough, exacting and complex doctrine, steeped in a drastic and uncompromising realism. And it is fatal to imagine that everybody knows quite well what Christianity is and needs only a little encouragement to practise it. The brutal fact is that in this Christian country not one person in a hundred has the faintest notion what the Church teaches about God or man or society or the person of Jesus Christ . . . Apart from a possible one per cent of intelligent and instructed Christians, there are three kinds of people we have to deal with. There are the frank and open heathen, whose notions of Christianity was a dreadful jumble of rags and tags of Bible anecdote and clotted mythological nonsense. There are the ignorant Christians, who combine a mild gentle-Jesus sentimentality with vaguely humanistic ethics—most of these are Arian heretics. Finally, there are the more or less instructed church-goers, who know all the arguments about divorce and auricular confession and communion in two kinds, but are about as well equipped to do battle on fundamentals against a Marxian atheist or a Wellsian agnostic as a boy with a pea-shooter facing a fan-fire of machine guns.

The reason for this state of affairs so far as it obtains in America is twofold. In America, Church and State are separated, so that religion is not taught in the public schools. Parents do not teach it any more in their homes, but leave it to the churches. The churches for the most part devote one hour on Sunday to Christian education—one hour—and the education is often terribly deficient in substance and quality.

The second part of the reason is that the culture and mental climate of our day are predominantly scientific. The minds of people are dominated by an all-pervading, secularized world view into which the thought of God scarcely enters. The tendency is to overlook the fact that there is a world above and beyond the senses, a world of spiritual values whose existence is no less real than the material world. Science has brought wonderful gains to humanity, but in what sense has it outmoded religion? Science and religion do not exclude each other; they mutually supplement each other. Great claims can be made for science, but not absolute, not totalitarian claims. It is one road to truth, but not the only one. It does not tell us all there is to know about life and the world. It deals with facts about physical nature and human nature, observable, verifiable facts. It classifies them, frames hypotheses to account for them, by experiment verifies or refutes the hypotheses, and so uncovers a system of universal laws, chemical, biological, psychological. But beyond this objective world with which science deals there are other facts, important and fundamental facts, which are inaccessible to the methods of science.

For example, what can science say about *love?* A mother writes to her two sons and tells each of them, "I give you all my love." What mathematics will take the measure of that? A man has casual sex relations with a number of women and then falls in love with a girl and marries her. The quality of the latter relationship is so different that the word "love" cannot be applied to both it and the earlier relationships. The thing that makes all the difference is precisely what cannot be analyzed scientifically. No amount of research in a laboratory will teach you what love is. You need another person to do that. And when you meet that person, you will learn what love is, not by any measurements or tests you may apply or by any psychological observations, however acute, but only by giving your heart, by committing yourself, which is a totally different attitude from that of measuring, weighing, and calculating. This was what Pascal was pointing to when he said, "The heart has its reasons which the reason knows not of."

What, moreover, can science tell us about *God?* Can God be the object of spatial and temporal measurements? The stars cannot be carted into a laboratory for close range study, but they can be seen through a telescope and analyzed by means of the spectroscope. God, on the other hand, being invisible and nonmaterial, cannot be observed or analyzed by the methods of science. You do not get to know Him in that fashion. You cannot manipulate Him.

Take the case of Jesus. Is anybody in his senses going to say that His teaching is old stuff or that science has outmoded Him? Is the Sermon on the Mount out of date, or the Golden Rule? We have still to catch up with Jesus. Yet He is never to be found arguing a case for the existence of God. He did not arrive at His knowledge of God as the result of scientific or philosophical inquiry. The truths He declared are not hypotheses tested by the scientist's method of trial and error. They are intuitively perceived by spiritual insight. As with Jesus, so with all who lay claim to religious experience. It is in the realm of faith and hope, of love and loyalty, that religious conviction is found. To be sure, these are intangibles, not susceptible to scientific techniques, but they are no less real and powerful. Consider the comment of Sir Arthur Eddington:

The materialist who is convinced that all phenomena arise from electrons and quanta and the like controlled by mathematical formulae, must presumably hold the belief that his wife is a rather elaborate differential equation; but he is probably tactful enough not to obtrude this opinion in domestic life. If this kind of scientific dissection is felt to be inadequate and irrelevant in *ordinary* personal relationships, it is surely out of place in the most personal relationship of all—that of the human soul to the Divine Spirit.

You see, then, what my reply would be to the woman who said: "We have no religion. My husband is a scientist." That is a "lulu" of a *non sequitur!* Science is one road to truth, but not the only one. It does not tell us all that there is to know about life and the world. When we are dealing with the inner world, the world of spirit, the world of freedom, decision, responsibility, the world of personal relationships where, after all, our needs are greatest, we cannot afford to dispense with the intuitions, insights, and certitudes of religion. The more men have concentrated on this world to the exclusion of any recognition of the eternal world, the more nearly they have come to turning this world not into a paradise but into a hell.

We are in the Space Age. Ours is a generation engrossed with the task of achieving mastery over the earth, sea, and sky. We are all caught up in the process and tend to forget that what is material is only one half of the full circle of life, and not the more important half. Don't omit the invisible in your reckoning. There is more to existence than you can touch, taste, and measure. There is more to the universe than earth and air and sky and sea. We live in two worlds, not one. There is a world beyond and yet within the visible world. There is a "Presence that disturbs us with the joy of elevated thoughts." There is a spiritual power which, working through human agents, has produced all that is noble in music, art, and literature. God is not far from any one of us. By all means listen to what the scientists have to say, but listen also to the psalmists and prophets, the saints and mystics, the poets and musicians. Listen above all to Jesus Christ, the greatest spiritual influence the world has ever known. He is not outmoded. He is the Master Light of all our seeing, the Way, the Truth, the Life. In every generation, men have called Him Teacher, Lord, Savior. For the transformation of our personal lives and the regeneration of society, we desperately need what He has to offer. To anyone disposed to think religion old stuff, outmoded by science, I commend the judgment of Dr. Arthur Compton, Nobel prize winner in physics: "Science has created a world in which Christianity is an imperative."

III

Isn't One Religion as Good as Another?

Talking with a student some time ago about religion, I made what he thought was an unwarranted claim for Christianity. He was not prepared to concede the claim. It did not seem to him that Christianity was unique or as supreme as I had suggested. His contention was that when all is said and done, one religion is as good as another.

It is an argument often advanced. The different religions—this is how it runs—have a lot in common. Their beliefs and the ideas of morality they inculcate are not strikingly dissimilar. In any case, even where there are deviations, each people has the religion best suited to its own race, climate, condition. If *we* had been born within a different culture we would have followed a different religion, and who is to say it would not have been the right religion for us?

Consider what relativism like this implies. Missionary propaganda is an impertinence. By what right do Christians seek to proselytize among Hindus? Why should an American go to Africa and urge a tribe by the Congo to forsake its ancestral faith? Are the peoples of the earth not all traveling at their own pace along their own roads to the same destination? Does it really matter what *form* of religion we profess? If we *live* by our faith isn't that what counts?

These are questions with which I shall deal farther on. But first let us note how they compare with the attitude common among Christians right up to the opening years of the twentieth century. So far from thinking that one religion was as good as another, the prevailing opinion for centuries was that there was only one true religion—Christianity—and all the others were false. Martin Luther called Mohammed "the

17

Devil's worshiper" and dismissed the Koran as "brutish and hoggish." In his famous hymn, "From Greenland's Icy Mountains," Bishop Reginald Heber had a line: "The heathen in his blindness bows down to wood and stone." The implication is that only Christians have seen the light, the rest of the world is in gross darkness. The good bishop drew no distinction between the fetish worship of backward tribes and the devout reverence of the Muslim prostrating himself before Allah, or the highest aspirations of Hindu and Buddhist saints. All alike were "heathen," "men benighted," and in "error's chain."

Before condemning this attitude outright we ought in fairness to remember that men like Bishop Heber wrote about non-Christian religions as they knew them, and not as we know them today. If the first missionaries were unsympathetic we can understand why. The only Hinduism with which they were familiar was a Hinduism which sanctioned the cruelties of widow-burning and infanticide and which was used to perpetuate the exploitation of the outcastes. They knew next to nothing of the mysticism of the Upanishads and the Bhagavad-Gita. And so with Buddhism, Confucianism, Shinto, and the other non-Christian faiths.

It was when the sacred books of the East were translated, and the religious treasures which they contain were brought to light, that the attitude of Christians to the historic religions changed. They learned that God had not left Himself in any land without a witness, that other faiths have saints and seers, that in their scriptures are lofty conceptions, deep searchings after truth. They became aware of that sense of the majesty of God and the consequent reverence in worship which is conspicuous in Islam; of the deep sympathy for the world's sorrow and the unselfish search for the way of escape from it, which are at the heart of Buddhism; of the desire for communion with Ultimate Reality, conceived as spiritual, which is prominent in Hinduism; of the belief in a moral order of the universe and the insistence on moral conduct which are such a marked feature of Confucianism. So it came about that the old classification, one religion true and all the others false,

was by more and more Christians abandoned, and George
Matheson could write the hymn:

> Gather us in: we worship only Thee;
> In varied names we stretch a common hand;
> In diverse forms a common soul we see;
> In many ways we seek one promised land.

However, from one extreme the pendulum has swung to
the other. Instead of the classification of religions as true and
false what one hears nowadays is that no religion is supreme
or unique, that they all contain much truth, the truth best
adapted to their adherents; and, therefore, that no attempt
should be made to get people to change their religion.
Gandhi, a man of deeply moral temperament, treated religion
with an easygoing relativism. He was a Hindu, and Hinduism, with millions of deities in its pantheon, is endlessly tolerant. It has at least six systems of religious philosophy, all
thoroughly incompatible and all irreproachably orthodox.
Radhakrishnan, the Hindu philosopher-statesman, adopts the
same position that Gandhi did.

> To obliterate every other religion than one's own [he has said] is
> a sort of Bolshevism in religion which we must try to prevent. We
> can do so only if we accept something like the Hindu solution, which
> sees the unity of religion not in a common creed but in a common
> quest. The world would be a much poorer thing, if one creed
> absorbed the rest. God wills a rich harmony and not a colorless
> uniformity.

This sounds plausible and makes a strong appeal to many
minds. People of good will want to see an end to the prejudice
and misunderstanding that create conflicts between the followers of different faiths. They deplore arrogance and im-
perialism in religion. But there is a tolerance that has its roots
not in faith but in a deep-seated skepticism. Despairing of
ever reaching ultimate truth, it holds that the most we can
do is make provisional hypotheses. This is why it is content to
have God named by any name. There is a tolerance of another

kind that has its roots in mental laziness. It simply will not
take the trouble to find out the facts. Without any justification whatever it reduces all the faiths to a common denomi-
nator. It repeats clichés like "One religion is as good as another," "You shouldn't criticize another person's religion," "It
makes little difference what your religion is so long as you
live up to it." As a rule, people who talk in such fashion pride
themselves on their tolerance whereas they should apologize
for their ignorance.

Such wild generalizations should not be allowed to go un-
contested. It is absurd to say that in the end all the religions
teach much the same thing. They have common elements, but
there are also deep cleavages. It is not for nothing that Hindus
and Muslims are so sorely divided, or Arabs and Jews. Will
anybody maintain that Christianity and Communism, the
youngest of the world's religions, teach much the same thing?
No right-thinking person wants to play up religious differences, but it can be misleading to minimize them, for they are
influential factors in the total world situation. By and large,
American Christians are muddled in their thinking about tolerance. Too many of them acquiesce too readily when it is
said that it makes little difference what your religion is so
long as you live up to it. It is one thing to recognize the right
of others to hold a faith different from your own. It is another
thing to take the position: What makes you a good Jew, and
you a good Arab, makes me a good Christian. When Christians employ such catch phrases, or acquiesce in them, they
show that their faith has been watered down into sentimentalism and humanitarianism. The real trouble is that they are
not so much tolerant as theologically illiterate or religiously
indifferent. It is the absence of positive conviction that accounts for such a compliant attitude.

It is, I hope, obvious that I am not advocating aggressive
antagonism among the world religions, still less the old dic-
tum that one religion is of God and all the others are of the
Devil. I believe that at one level there can be a fellowship between Christians, Hindus, Muslims, Jews—the level where all

together are seeking God, stretching out to Him hands of prayer. If only we could unite as seekers, in sympathy and with the desire to help one another, how much nearer the Kingdom of God would be. This is something we must strive for, whether by World Parliaments of Religion, or International Fellowships, or personal friendships, or by whatever way is open to us. But we have to remain loyal to the truth we have received. The differences between us—Jesus leading men to the Father, Buddha silent about God—are not obliterated by being slurred over or enveloped in a haze of sentimentalism. If the differences are slight, there is no case for Christian missions. If they are considerable, the question is whether they are differences in degree or in kind, which in turn throws us back on the question: What is the distinctive claim we make for Christianity?

First, there is its conception of God. Our claim is that in the lofty ethical monotheism of the Christian faith may be found the climax and consummation of man's whole commerce with the Supernatural. Christianity has taken up and made its own the noble passages in which the prophets of Israel declared the incomparable majesty and holiness of God. But these are not so asserted as to make fellowship with God impossible for man. Jesus taught His disciples to pray "Hallowed be Thy Name," but He first taught them to say "Our Father." And Father for Him signified the essential kinship of man with God and the great truth that God has made us in His image and that it is this indeed which constitutes us men. Since all men are His offspring, His children, fellowship with Him is possible. "Father" signified for Jesus that God is knowable, understandable, lovable. This is the Christian answer to the question asked in every country and in every century: What is God like? It is either true or false. If it is false we may not claim validity for it anywhere. If it is true it is good news for the whole world, and those of us who believe it and who profess to live by it and expect to die in it have no right to keep it to ourselves but must take active measures through the agency of Christian missions, as well as by personal testimony and advocacy, to share it.

The first distinctive claim we make for Christianity is its lofty conception of God. The second is the fact of Christ. When we are asked how we know that what we believe about God is true we point to Jesus Christ who believed it, taught it, lived it. He is the highest expression of God we have ever seen. In His life and teaching, His Cross and Resurrection, we believe we have found a moral and spiritual ultimate. We have come to a fixed point in our moral and spiritual universe. We know what life ought to be. We realize that if we are to be seriously religious we must be religious after the mind and spirit of Jesus. In Jesus, we have seen what God is like. He revealed the Father not only in His words but in His life and death and victory over death. The message of Christianity, therefore, is not a formula; it is a person. Its ideal is expressed not in a succession of commandments but in the character of One who lived and died as the type of all perfection. The righteousness and love of God are incarnate in Him. The child who was asked, "What is God like?" put her finger on a unique aspect of Christian faith when she replied, "God is like Jesus."

"Call Him a man," says Stanley Jones, "and you will have to change your ideas of what man is; call Him God, and you will have to change your ideas of what God is." Discussing the nature of God, a young theologian said, "The Christian thought of God has always had mystery at its center." His companion, the wiser of the two, revised this judgment: "No. The Christian thought of God has always had mystery at its periphery. But at its center, the face of Jesus Christ." If you want to know, so far as you may know, the nature of God, turn to the Person of Jesus. The power of a personal ideal is immeasurably greater than a set of abstract moral principles. Christianity has made love of Christ the supreme virtue, and it has proved the source and inspiration of all other virtues. Love of Christ always results in a growing likeness to Christ. Moreover, it brings the Christian into vital union with Christ and thereby communicates new life and character.

So we come to a third distinctive claim which we make for Christianity. It not only tells us what it is right to do, it undertakes to enable us to do it. It not only provides moral insight but moral power. This is man's immemorial need. When he has lived with any seriousness of thought and purpose he has always gone out in search of a spiritual dynamic. In all the religions he is to be found saying: "You have described the good life. Will you show me how I can begin and continue to live it?" Christianity's reply is to point to Christ. Its name for Him is not Sage but Savior. Its claim is that in Him there is power to produce and sustain character.

This is more than a claim. It has been demonstrated as fact in everyday experience right down the centuries. For those who wholeheartedly put their faith in Christ, who really commit their lives to Christ, the thing happens. They discover that to be a Christian is not simply to repeat a creed but to have a Savior whom they can trust completely and love supremely, who is always drawing out in them their best nature and making them resolve to be true to it; who looks into their eyes when they betray Him, so that they are ashamed; who imparts the forgiveness of sins and gives strength to live in fellowship with God. Apart from this, His ideal would mean only a new despair. But His strength is made perfect in weakness.

Here is the distinctive claim we make for Christianity. When it loses its power to convert, to remake and transform character, it loses its right to be called Christianity. The mark of a vital Christianity is that it introduces men and women to Christ the Savior, who can make the weak strong, the selfish unselfish, the unclean clean, who can make men and women lacking any real sense of God into men and women radiant in the consciousness of the Divine presence, grace, and power.

Asked by a Hindu why he and his wife had come to India, a young missionary replied: "We are here because Christlike character is the highest that we know, because Christ gives men a free, full life, and, most important of all, He gives them

God. And we do not know of anyone else who does do these things except Christ." Is there any better way of describing the mission of the Christian Church and, if we are church members, our part in it?

IV

When Trouble Comes

When Job's troubles were at their height, when he was
bereft of his sons and his property and afflicted with loath-
some sores from the sole of his foot to the crown of his head,
his wife said to him: "Do you still hold fast your integrity?
Curse God, and die."

It is extraordinary that a woman should have said that. No
doubt there was provocation. Her husband was a good man,
yet calamity had overwhelmed him. His plight was so desperate that she had given up hope of betterment for him, had
come to feel that anything, even death itself, was to be preferred to the misery he was in. Bewildered, resentful, heart-
broken, she bade him vent his bitterness on God and be done
with life.

That a woman should have let herself go in such fashion is
extraordinary. Women, it has been said, are wiser than men
because though they may know less they understand more.
They are frequently referred to as the weaker sex. The weaker
sex! A man in suffering is sometimes a child and often a baby;
a woman, called upon to suffer, can be very strong. Maarten
Maartens, the Dutch novelist, wrote to a friend: "Look at my
wife—always racked by rheumatism in the head, always
bright. Women can do that sort of thing. Had Job been a
woman there would have been no Book of Job for she would
simply have sat down in the muckheap and said, 'How good
God is!' " A gallant but curious comment. Maartens had apparently forgotten all about Job's wife and her derisive out-
burst, "Curse God, and die."

In calamity, that is how some instinctively react. Their
minds turn at once to God; their feelings toward Him are

harsh and rebellious. Lord Londonderry set down this entry in his journal: "Here I learned that Almighty God, for reasons best known to Himself, had been pleased to burn down my house in the county of Durham." A man whose three children were killed when a schoolhouse collapsed screamed curses against God because of their death. He did not know at the time that the schoolhouse had not been built properly for an earthquake area, that to save money shoddy material was used, that back of his personal tragedy was a corrupt and inefficient local government. A soldier, fatally wounded an hour or two before the Armistice of World War I, his fondest hopes quenched at the last moment, said, "Isn't it like God to do a thing like this?" If you have read Thomas Hardy's *Tess of the D'Urbervilles* there is little chance that you will forget a sentence in the concluding paragraph: "The President of the Immortals had ended his sport with Tess."

When men blaspheme it is not God but the false God who has been presented to them whom they reject and curse. Pascal said that it is the pathetic fate of God to be everlastingly misunderstood. The leader of a Bible class of miners in England always began each year's study of the Scriptures with the stipulation: "Whatever we think or say, boys, let us be sure we keep clear the character of God." How right he was! People harbor such false and unworthy ideas of God; directly attribute to Him wars, epidemics, diseases; speak of Him as "sending," as "willing," these evils; call them "acts of God." A British clergyman wrote in the press that God had "sent" World War II to punish the nation for having allowed the Welsh Church to be disestablished! A girl, suffering from an affliction of the eye, went to see a specialist and was told that she must lose her sight. "Is God going to take away my eyes?" she at once exclaimed. Back of these admittedly exceptional cases there is a very widespread impression of a God who is not only strict and demanding but implacable, vindictive, revengeful.

Let me say emphatically that such a God should be blasphemed. He is a caricature of the God and Father of our Lord

Jesus Christ. How can people worship such a God or trust Him? In their hearts they are bound to fear Him, to seek to appease Him, to resent and shun rather than love and serve Him. Martin Luther wrote a great deal about the enmity of man towards God. It is often an unconscious, perhaps sub-conscious, enmity, and who can doubt that it has been fed and nourished by misconceptions of the nature and character of God? Revolting against the view that God had deliberately caused the war of 1914, had deliberately brought the awful agony of it on mankind as a punishment for the sins of ir-religion, drunkenness, impurity, Studdert-Kennedy wrote:

> And I hate the God of Power on His hellish heavenly throne,
> Looking down on rape and murder, hearing little children moan.

Again,

> Are there no tears in the heart of the Eternal?
> Is there no pain to pierce the soul of God?
> Then must He be a fiend of Hell infernal,
> Beating the earth to pieces with His rod.

Intemperate language, you say, but take into account what goaded Studdert-Kennedy to resort to it. When men blas-pheme it is not God but the false God who has been presented to them whom they reject and curse.

One of the great weaknesses of our religious life is the in-adequacy of our conception of God. We have not found with our minds a God worthy of worship, a God we can relate to the scientific age, a God who commands our intellectual re-spect as well as the homage of our hearts and the obedience of our lives. The weakness is most marked where the character of God is concerned. For great numbers of us, He is an ex-acting Overlord, an inscrutable and implacable Power. More than anything else, what we need to have Christianized is our thinking about God. God should not be conceived as *sending* evil. Calamity is not His deliberate handiwork. Dis-ease is not of His making.

The Institute of Physical Medicine and Rehabilitation in New York City is a grim place—broken necks, broken backs, arms dangling and useless, legs horribly misshapen, speech halting, labored, and broken. Are you going to dare tell me that all this is God's doing? Can you believe that God deliberately *wills* that a bright girl of 19, a lover of outdoor sports and of dancing, should develop polio and lie for months with twisted useless limbs? If one *wills* anything one *wants* it to happen. No one but a fiend could look on a crippled person and say, "This is what I wanted to happen." For my own part, I would not worship or trust or serve a God like that for five minutes, and to love Him would be impossible.

Job, though bewildered and mystified by the trouble that came upon him, did not curse God. "Though he slay me, yet will I trust him," was his cry. What intrepid heroism! What selfless devotion! That cry has brought courage and resolution to many an afflicted soul. And yet, its premise has to be rejected. "Though he slay me"—will God, whose name and nature are love, whose heart is most wonderfully kind, do what no father in his senses would dream of doing, what he would rightly be sent to prison for doing?

It is to Jesus we should turn in such matters. He proclaimed God's fatherly rule over all His children. He taught that no sparrow falls to the ground without the Father's knowledge, that God clothes the lilies, feeds the ravens, numbers the very hairs of our heads, sends His sun and rain, His unconditioned bounty and kindness, upon good and bad, the thankful and the thankless. He taught us to pray "Thy will be done," but a cloud of misconception surrounds that prayer. All sorts of lies have been told about it, and all manner of evils have been tolerated under its protection. Far too many people, when they pray "Thy will be done," think of lonely grief, wasting sickness, premature death. Christ would have us think of the will of God in positive ways. God's will means *health*. He wants disease to be conquered. A great part of our Lord's time was spent in healing the sick. He cannot have thought that disease was the will of God. God's will means *happy homes.* Slums cannot be the will of God. Hideous dwellings like those in lower East Harlem cannot be any part of His design. He has put us into the world to make it a home for His children. It is His will that we should go to work to clean it up. God's will means *not war but peace.* It cannot be His intention that men should manufacture deadly explosives like the nuclear weapons with which the Great Powers are experimenting. We should be careful how we speak of the will of God. Why should "Thy will be done," be a moan of resignation? Why should it suggest only graveyards, disease, calamity? We should associate it with health and happiness and abounding vitality.

I am not suggesting that this will solve all our problems. We may not think of God as *sending* trouble and tragedy, but the fact remains that He *permits* them, that they exist in a world made by Him, that they are a substantial ingredient in all our lives. We may not say, "Why has God done this to me?" but instinctively when trouble comes we ask, "Why did this have to happen?" If the terrible evils that befall us could be explained altogether in terms of human ignorance, folly, and sin, the problem would be solved in great measure, but there are disasters that defy explanation, baffling and bewildering us by their mysteriousness. I am reminded of the surgeon who said that if he appeared before the Most High he would present Him with a cancerous bone and ask Him for an explanation. It is the calamity that befalls others, not the calamity that befalls ourselves, that raises the deepest questions. It is when we see innocent children and men and women who are the soul of goodness suffer that faith is strained most, and it comes home to us that the world is not patently the creation of a loving and beneficent God.

How to reconcile the griefs and graves of men with the goodness and fatherliness of God—that is the problem. And Christianity, if anything, sharpens it. The noblest soul the world has ever known, betrayed, deserted, scourged, spat upon, crucified—that is the problem. Phillips Brooks once remarked that if someone should tell him that he could explain the mystery of evil, he would close his ears to the offer. Brooks knew that when all has been said that may be said—the existence of good as well as evil, the amount of suffering due to sin and ignorance, the educative value of suffering; the world a school for character, a vale of soul-making, not a lotus-eater's paradise—there remains a dark mystery that cannot be fathomed.

Well, what after all is faith? It is "the assurance of things hoped for, the conviction of things not seen." In essence faith is always a going against appearances. It is an assent to something about which you cannot prove that it is impossible that you should be mistaken. It is not belief in spite of evidence; it is belief in scorn of circumstance; it is the resolve to stand or fall by the noblest hypothesis. Trust in God, and much of existence is still a riddle. Faith is needed if we are to hold that all is for the best, the faith of a Whittier:

> Yet, in the maddening maze of things,
> And tossed by storm and flood,
> To one fixed stake my spirit clings;
> I know that God is good!

Besides, if there were nothing to try our faith in God, it might become shallow, flabby, feeble. But when pressed and tried by the sore problems of life it can become deep and strong. It is with faith as with virtue; it needs to be tested like steel in the fires of temptations and difficulties.

Long ago a wise and good man said, "This is the victory that overcomes the world, our faith." His belief in God, what he believed about God, the convictions he held about the character of God, enabled him to rise above every adverse circumstance and master it. Another great soul, no stranger to trouble, plagued by a crippling, humiliating handicap which he called a "thorn in the flesh," "a messenger of Satan" sent to buffet him, and which he repeatedly prayed might be removed but which was not removed, so that he had to come to terms with it and make friends with it till the day he died, volunteered this testimony: "We are handicapped on all sides but we are never frustrated; we are puzzled, but never in despair. We are persecuted, but we never have to stand it alone: we may be knocked down but we are never knocked out!"

How courageous men and women are made by faith in the God and Father of our Lord Jesus Christ! How strong and calm and resolute! Doubt paralyzes. It drains the energies, depletes the resources, takes the heart out of us. On the other hand, faith vitalizes. It supplies energy, increases resource, puts heart into us. This is no secondhand story I am bringing to you. This is not something read in a book or advanced as a theory. This is something you yourself can prove in your own experience. Multitudes have done so. In dark and difficult days one thing has kept them on their feet, has saved them from the loss of nerve, has kept them free from cynicism and self-pitying complaint—their faith in God. Out of pastoral—and personal—experience I can testify that there is no misfortune, no tragedy, no burden of sorrow or sickness so great but a believing soul can come out on top of it a conqueror, more than a conqueror.

You know how it is. For years we maintain the even tenor of our way through life. Everything goes well with us, goes so well that we take it all for granted: health, happiness, work, the ability to do our work. And then, sometimes with appalling suddenness, we are in deep waters and sorrows like sea billows roll. What we need in such an hour is an anchor of the soul, sure and steadfast, something we can hold on to, something that will keep a strong hold on us and not let us go or let us down, something stable, dependable, its foundations firm and immovable. The need can be supplied. We are not alone. We are never alone. We are more than conquerors through Him that loved us. Through Him—it is not a case of bracing ourselves, whistling to keep our courage up, bidding ourselves play the man, rallying such interior resources as we can muster of pluck and perseverance. It is rather that morning by morning we turn to God saying, "Strong Deliverer, be Thou still my Strength and Shield," and never turn in vain. "This is the victory that overcomes the world, our faith."

V

Why Go to Church?

Many who feel the need of a personal religion are impatient with institutional religion. They incline to the one and ignore the other. All that matters, they say, is that a person should win his way sincerely and thoughtfully to his own religious convictions and strive to model his conduct in accordance with them.

It is recorded of Jesus that "he went to the synagogue, as his custom was, on the sabbath day." The statement is made in passing, but it is noteworthy because of what it tells us about the personal habits of Jesus. He was scrupulous in His observance of the public worship of God. He knew, none better than He, that God can be worshiped anywhere. He could have found ample support for His religious life in quiet meditation, private prayer, under the open sky.

> When He walked the fields He drew
> From the flowers and birds and dew,
> Parables of God.

Nevertheless, on the day in the week set apart for public worship He was always in His place in the house of God. He could say with the psalmist: "How amiable are thy tabernacles, O Lord of hosts! My soul longeth, yea, even fainteth for the courts of the Lord: . . . For a day in thy courts is better than a thousand."

It is strange to think of Jesus being preached to Sabbath after Sabbath. What were the preachers like? Was what they had to say interesting, relevant, inspiring? Were they wise, good, godly men? Or were they an embodiment of all that He had afterwards to denounce in Pharisee and scribe? We don't

32

know enough to be sure of the answer, though there is a good deal to suggest that the preaching was often dull and the services usually formal, conventional, uninspiring. The fact of the matter is that the character of the service did not affect His attendance. For Him the house of God was a spiritual home. It was a necessity for the cultivation of the soul. It provided an opportunity of contributing as well as receiving religious experience. He was a lover of the house of God. He was to be found there without fail Sabbath after Sabbath.

Protestants by and large are rather casual in their attitude toward church attendance. For many it is incidental, optional, in no sense regarded as obligatory. They do not take it seriously or look upon it as an essential part of a Christian's duty and privilege. Inner attitude, they sometimes say, is what matters, not outward observance, the result being that outward observance is minimized, and on occasion disparaged. "Spiritual religion," it is maintained, is what really counts, and it is independent of forms and ceremonies. Comments run all the way from "Can't I worship God in the green fields?" to "I don't go to church because I see no point in it." The people offering the comments reckon themselves religious, but feel that their time can be more profitably employed than in churchgoing and their soul fed in other and indeed better ways.

One important consideration, however, they overlook. Inner attitude is the vital thing in religion, but it should not be divorced from outward observance. We Protestants say that religion is a transaction between an individual and his Maker and that no form or ceremony is necessary. God can be worshiped without intermediaries or accessories anywhere and at any time. We have the highest authority for saying what we do. When the woman of Samaria told Jesus, "Our fathers worshiped on this mountain; and you say that in Jerusalem is the place where men ought to worship," His reply was, "Believe me, the hour is coming when neither on this mountain nor in Jerusalem will you worship the Father. . . . God is spirit, and those who worship him must worship in spirit and in truth." The emphasis there is on inner attitude. Worship can rise spontaneously, without external aids, without set days and seasons. It can be offered alone, and when and where it seems most natural: in the quietness of one's own room, among the mountains, amid the din and bustle of city streets. Forms, ceremonies, services are not absolutely indispensable to religion, but this is not to say that they are alien to it, or that they hamper and impede it, or that they are of little consequence. On the contrary, they are the God-given means to secure the end, to promote religion. "Means of grace" our forebears called them. The mistake Jews and Samaritans alike made was to turn the means into ends. They put the major emphasis on outward observance and forgot the primary necessity of inner attitude. It is not the mistake of our generation. We fail to achieve the end because we neglect the means.

Calvin Coolidge's answer to the question "Can't I worship God in the green fields?" was characteristically brief and brusque: "You can, but you don't." Like all sweeping statements it does not take exceptions into account, but it underscores the broad, general fact of the matter. In a small mountain town in Kentucky a young minister made a somewhat unusual funeral announcement from his pulpit. He was just about to move to another charge, perhaps because he was given to making just such unusual announcements. He said, "The funeral of Mr. John Brown will be held from this church tomorrow afternoon at three o'clock. And Mr. Brown will be here himself, in person, for the first time in three years." Mr. Brown had been neglectful of outward observance. Is it a fair presumption that he had been even more neglectful of inner attitude?

Because Protestants by and large are too casual in their attitude to public worship, the onus is on Protestant preachers to do more often what their Roman Catholic brethren do with great regularity. It is to indicate why, in the words of the writer of the Epistle to the Hebrews, we should not neglect "to meet together, as is the habit of some."

For one thing, there is the public recognition we owe to God.

Worship is our apprehension of something so superior to our highest self that it calls forth our admiration, awe, and love. It is first and foremost the tribute of man to his Maker, of the finite to the Infinite, of the imperfect to the Perfect, of the sinful to the Holy. "Our Father, who art in heaven, hallowed be Thy Name"—that fundamentally is what worship means. It is what arises in the heart when God ceases to be an object of speculation, a subject for argument, and becomes for us the absolute Reality. "I come to seek God because I need Him," may be an adequate formula for prayer. "I come to adore His splendor, and cast myself and all I have at His feet" is the only possible formula for worship. During one of the darkest periods of World War II, William Temple, then Archbishop of Canterbury, said in a broadcast to America:

> I am disposed to begin by making what many people will feel to be a quite outrageous statement. The world can be saved from political chaos and collapse by one thing only, and that is worship. For to worship is to quicken the conscience by the holiness of God, to feed the mind with the truth of God, to purge the imagination by the beauty of God, to open up the heart to the love of God, to devote the will to the purpose of God. We go to church to worship God.

We go, too, because we need what the Church exists to provide—insight into life's meanings, control over life's circumstances, inward power for life's moral purposes. We slip out of the press of things, turn from the roar and rumble of the constant traffic of the world into the house of God, to restore our souls, to keep our vision and courage and love for people, to lay hold upon the grace and power of Christ. We go to church for moral cleansing, spiritual enrichment, new perspectives. In church we are reminded of something finer, greater, more enduring than the preoccupations of the common day. We are not only engineers, doctors, tradesmen, teachers, secretaries, lawyers, but children of God and heirs of immortality.

No lover of New York City, no one who has at heart the best interests of its citizens, would think of proposing that Central

Park should be parceled out to merchants and tradesmen and made into a thriving, commercial area. As Central Park is a reservation in space, so Sunday should be a reservation in time, a day on which by attendance at church and the assistance of "the means of grace" we breathe a clearer air, walk with a firmer tread, see life steadily and see it whole. The tower of a church rises above the homes and institutions by which it is surrounded, and points like a great finger to the sky. It is a sermon in stone. It preaches eloquently seven days a week of man's aspirations after a higher life. Were all the churches to be closed, and men and women never to meet together as religious beings, it would be as though the reservoir that supplies a great city with water suddenly ran dry. On this point, Dr. Harry Emerson Fosdick, preaching from the pulpit of Riverside Church, once said:

> Here in this church today, with the great tradition of the Christian heritage around us, with Christ's way of life exalted above the sordid level of our vulgar world, with God calling us to lift up our eyes unto the hills from whence cometh our help, we are all within reach of wealth for our souls, which can make us resourceful, secure, confident, dedicated, strong. Don't miss it.

We come to church also because of the fellowship to be found there. Christianity stands for a social view of man. It is in the world to create fellowship, of man with man as well as of man with God. It requires, therefore, fellowship in worship as in other activities. How, then, can a man be a Christian who insists that all his highest moments shall be unsocial, that he can only find and feel and reverence God in solitariness, segregated from his brother men? In Scotland, a story has long been current concerning a member of a Highland parish who went about saying that he could find God as well in his garden and on the mountainside as he could by attending church on Sunday. One day his minister called on him and was invited to sit by the fireside. The parishioner knew that the minister must have noticed his absence from church. He suspected that he had heard on what grounds he had been justifying his nonchurchgoing, and anticipated that he was going to be taken to task on both counts. They sat in silence for a time. Then the minister rose, went to the fireplace, took the tongs, and lifting a single coal from the embers placed it alone on the hearth. It quickly turned into a black ash while the fire in the fireplace continued to glow and give forth heat. The head of the house then spoke up. "You needn't say a word. I understand what you mean. I'll be in my place at church next Sunday."

It is a privilege to be able to seek God alone. On the Christian view it is our clear duty to go to God together. Besides being a duty, worshiping together is a spiritual help, just because we have in fact the social nature which Christianity calls upon us to strengthen. We shall miss a great deal if we always go to God singly. Just as, though we can be happy alone, some forms of happiness can only be had in company, so, though we can and sometimes ought to worship alone, some parts of the fullness of worship can only be realized in community, in the felt presence of fellow believers. When we are not in the mood for worship, the social bond with others who are, can pull us into it; when we are in the mood, that same bond gives to our worshiping overtones, subtle additions of volume, that can come in no other way. To take an imperfect analogy, how very much more we can enter into the spirit of great music when we listen to an orchestra with a hushed multitude in a public hall than when we listen to a recording alone!

What makes a church magnetic? The spirit that pervades it—the warmth, the vitality, the fellowship, especially the fellowship. William Blake said that the lack of fellowship is hell. Dickens' Bill Sykes, the murderer of Nancy, couldn't stay away from London because, as he put it, "There's somebody there I can talk to." The human heart hungers for fellowship. There are many ways of creating it—identity of interest, devotion to a common cause, affinity of nature and need—but there are none so binding and so lasting as the links forged between human beings on the basis of a common approach to God. In

worship, men meet at the deepest level of life, and where God
and man draw close together, at that point men draw nearer
to one another.

Some years ago I preached in St. Martin's Church, London.
It was a memorable experience. Situated in Trafalgar Square,
right in the heart of the city, it is a historic old church. Its services are always crowded. Its vicars have been outstanding.
Its record of social service is unique. What has made it magnetic? Its fellowship. One who knows it well has described it.

> Hundreds of thousands of men, for whom religion had meant
> routine, boredom, mumbo-jumbo, something desiccated and dead,
> found it was exciting, moving, helpful, alive. St. Martin's Church be-
> came . . . the church of the classes and the masses; . . . the church
> for the cheerful and the church for the desperate; the church for the
> healthy and the sick; of the young and the old. It was a church in
> which the congregation was no more shocked at hearing the minister
> pray for the streetwalkers than for schoolteachers, . . . for black-
> guards than for bishops. . . . It became a refuge for the unhappy,
> and the home of the homeless. In short, it was a Christian fellowship.

Why go to church? To find and foster fellowship. To acquire insight into life's meanings, control over life's circumstances, inward power for life's moral purposes. To worship
and bow down before our Maker, to join with "the whole congregation of faithful people dispersed throughout the world"
in saying, "We praise Thee, O God; we acknowledge Thee to
be the Lord."

VI

Putting Our Brains to Work in the Service of Religion

When Jesus said, ". . . you shall love the Lord your God with all . . . your mind," He affirmed emphatically that there is a place in religion for the exercise of the intelligence. God wants our heads as well as our hearts. We gather in church for worship, and our aesthetic sense is quickened by the beauty of line and stone which is all around us, our emotions are stirred as accompanied by choir and organ we sing in unison the great hymns of the church—but our minds should be kindled too. When Schleiermacher in the classroom at the University of Berlin kept reiterating that feeling was the basic, constitutive element in religion, Hegel, through the wall from him, would expostulate, *"Aber, meine Herren, das Denken ist auch Gottesdienst."* To think, and to think hard, is a religious duty. For Hegel, devoting one's mind to the service of God was every bit as necessary as private prayer or public worship. Was he not right? When God claims a man, He claims the whole man, his brains included.

Look into the story of the Church. What would have become of Christianity had it not been for the thinkers—in the first century men like Paul and John and the unknown author of the Epistle to the Hebrews, in the second and third centuries men like the great Alexandrian Fathers, Clement and Origen? They never made a virtue of ignorance or credulity. They labored to commend the Christian faith to the intelligence of their contemporaries. They honored the mind as the instrument that apprehends and appropriates truth. They were abreast of the best thinking of their age. Soon they were more than abreast of it; they were the intellectual leaders of their day. Dr. John Knox is no more than stating the facts when he writes:

> Christianity began magnificently. It stepped from the soil of Palestine on its westward march with the tread of a conqueror. . . . It did not sit at philosophy's feet; philosophy was soon sitting at its feet. For all its humble origin among Galilean peasants and working men—poor and unschooled—it became the teacher of Greece as it became the ruler of Rome.

So it has been in every creative period of the Church's life. When men put their brains to work in the service of God things begin to happen. First you have the Revival of Learning and then, as inevitably as day follows night, you have the Reformation. First you have a stirring in the minds of John and Charles Wesley, both of them university men, and then you have the Evangelical Revival which sweeps through England like a flame of fire, cleansing life at every level, personal, political, social, and ecclesiastical. First you have a youth in Buffalo intellectually coming of age, finding many of the traditional views of the Bible untenable, distressed by the discovery and obliged because of it to go out in search of a personal faith, a faith that would scorn to tamper with truth and that would do no violence to his intelligence. Then for over forty years you have the ministry of Dr. Harry Emerson Fosdick, a ministry unparalleled in this generation, reaching out through the spoken and written word literally to millions of people, clarifying their thinking about the things that matter most, resolving their intellectual difficulties, building them up in the faith that God is Truth.

Yes, great things begin to happen when men put their brains to work in the service of religion. Who have been the commanding figures in the history of the Church? Call the roll and what do you find? They have been men of intellectual strength—Paul, Athanasius, Augustine, Aquinas, Calvin, Temple—men who regarded the mind not only as a useful instrument but as a sacred instrument to be devoted to the glory of God and in the furtherance of His purposes.

If only that were the whole story! Unfortunately there is another side to it. Far from regarding the mind as a sacred instrument there are some who distrust it. A man went into a church and heard the preacher say in the course of the sermon: "Few things, my friends, have done more harm in this world than thought." He then proceeded, though it was surely quite unnecessary: "Don't, my dear friends, put me down as a thinker, put me down as a believer." But that is a false antithesis. What is the value of belief without thought? Belief without thought is superstition. It is the acceptance of opinions at second hand and on hearsay. In religion, the second hand is intolerable, yet how much religious life is the echo of an echo. Thousands are alienated from Christianity because going to church means listening to a sermon in which thought is divorced from feeling, a sermon that insults their intelligence.

This distrust of reason has all along been widespread. Plutarch tells us that when he went to his father with questions about religion, all that he could get from him was "The ancient faith is enough; if you begin to criticize, there is no knowing where you will stop." The words were spoken hundreds of years ago, but they have a familiar ring. "Ask no questions about religion. What was good enough for your forebears ought to be good enough for you. Questions are dangerous." Plutarch was not put off by such an evasive reply. No person of independent mind would be. One thing he should refuse to do; he should refuse to cheat about his religion. He is not going to be asked to put up with old-fashioned science or old-fashioned business methods. Why should he be asked to make a fetish of old-fashioned religion?

When Robertson Smith was on trial for heresy and making a spirited defense of his position at the bar of the General Assembly of the Church of Scotland, an elder of the Church, a good, devout man who by profession was a lawyer, expressed himself thus: "Granted that Robertson Smith is right, if it is truth, it is dangerous truth, and he has no right as a professor of the Church to upset the Church by declaring it." He was overheard by a lad who was in his freshman year at Edinburgh University, a lad who thought that the pursuit of truth, the whole truth and nothing but the truth, was a religious duty. He said that had he been then intending to enter the ministry he would probably have been put off it by the elder's attitude, but that instead it served as a call to his life's work—the search for truth which would shine in its own light in the face of all inquiry. The lad was John Oman, who was later to write one of the best books about the Christian religion—*Vision and Authority*—to appear in his generation.

Notice what the effects are of this distrust of reason. A schism is set up between the heart and the head. There is an attempt to fetter free inquiry and to keep belief fixed and static. Can you imagine a scientist clinging tenaciously to outworn expressions of belief? The scientist is, like Socrates, ready to follow truth wherever it leads and to give up the most venerable of ideas once it is demonstrated that the truth is not in them. Christians who believe that God is a God of truth should be no less openminded. If people have fantastically fuzzy ideas about God, if they are bewildered and puzzled as to what they should believe and why, if the attitude of nine persons out of ten to Christianity is a sort of inert agnosticism, the reason is not far to seek. They have not brought the same intellectual interest to religion that they have to the other concerns of life. Enterprising in most fields of endeavor, they are indolent in this. They have not learned to love God with all their mind.

A remark made by a church member years ago has stayed with me. "I am," he said, "a Free Mason high up in my order, and what I know of Masonry today is quite a different thing from what I knew ten years ago. But I cannot say that there is much about my faith which I did not know twenty years ago." Progressive Masonry, static churchmanship. And why? Because in the one case you have keen interest, deep attachment, while in the other you have a relationship which somehow has done nothing to alert or engage the mind. Of how many of us is that the story? The apprehension of God has not kept abreast of our other apprehensions. We pride ourselves on being informed about most things, yet we let our spiritual life stand still. Mature in all else, in religion we remain at the childish stage.

How, for example, do we think about God? Have we done anything to purge our minds of crude and childish conceptions of Him? A student in answer to a questionnaire wrote: "I think of God as real, actual skin and blood and bones, something we shall see with our eyes some day, no matter what lives we lead on earth." For a child to think of God in such fashion is natural, but no adult should be content to entertain notions as immature or unworthy. What about our prayers? There are men and women who have carried over from childhood a form of words which they use still, with little thought for its meaning and relevance, and sometimes with little genuine belief that it has a Hearer. They pray partly in conformity to long-established habit, partly as an emotional need, and also because they believe there may be some kind of telepathic influence, but their minds are not brought into any kind of vigorous action. They resemble Mundanus, as William Law describes him.

Mundanus is a man of excellent parts and clear apprehension. He is well advanced in age and has made a great figure in business. Every part of trade that has fallen in his way has had some improvement from him, and he is always contriving to carry any method of doing anything well to its greatest height. . . . The only thing which has not fallen under his improvement, nor received any benefit from his judicious mind is his devotion. This is in just the same poor state as it was when he was only six years of age, and the old man prays now in that little form of words which his mother used to hear him repeat night and morning.

About such a state of affairs there is only one thing to say. When a man keeps his secular interests always on the move and lets his religious life stand still, it is not to be wondered at that it shrinks from a major concern to a minor detail and that the practice of it ceases to be a joy and becomes solely a duty, if even that.

Many people today are dissatisfied with their religion. They have good reason to be dissatisfied with it. It is substantially the religion of their childhood. Much of it consists of vague memories of what they were taught at Sunday School. They are competent at business, wide awake as to what is happening in the world, conscientious and forward-looking in their citizenship, but in their knowledge of Christianity they have made no advances. A man with whom I recently had a discussion about Christianity credited it with conceptions many of which may have been current years ago but which no literate Christian entertains today. Since he was a student of physics I could not refrain from asking what he would think of me if in what I had to say about science I betrayed that I knew nothing of its recent or current developments. The look that came over his face was more expressive than the answer I got.

If I am describing the position of any reader, I urge him to study the fundamentals of the Christian religion, to apply his mind to Christian ethics and their relation to the problems of national and international life. I urge him to read a book like *The Meaning of Faith* by Dr. Harry Emerson Fosdick, or *Christian Behavior* by C. S. Lewis, or *The Ethical Teaching of Jesus* by E. F. Scott or *International Conflict in the Twentieth Century* by Herbert Butterfield. At any rate, one must give Christianity a chance before criticizing or rejecting it. It is necessary to understand what it is and what it offers.

So I come back to the first and great commandment. ". . . you shall love the Lord your God with all your heart, and with all your soul, *and with all your mind,* and with all your strength." There is a place in religion for the exercise of the intelligence. God wants our heads as well as our hearts. To think, and to think hard, is a religious duty. How one wishes that more men and women would give their brains to the service of religion and do it with something like the diligence and devotion that fill their days from Monday until Friday. How one wishes that more of the daring and enterprise, the grasp of essentials, the power of initiative, the directness of decision, that mark the world of business could find their way into the life and work of the Church.

To people who are able and gifted, their minds disciplined and effective instruments, I say: Are you putting your brain to work in the service of religion? You recognize it to be an indispensable tool. Do you recognize it as something else, as sacred, as an instrument to be consecrated, to be given back to God who gave it to you? The person for whom that is a discovery has a double offering to make to God.

> Oh God, I offer Thee my heart—
> In many a mystic mood, by beauty led,
> I give my heart to Thee. But now impart
> That sterner grace—to offer Thee my head.

VII

God and Outer Space

Christian belief is set the task today of relating itself to the vast, uncomprehended reaches of the universe to whose existence science is making us profoundly sensitive. The Ptolemaic astronomy has long since been discarded. The old three-level cosmogony—heaven, earth, hell—is a thing of the past. What have we put in their place? A friend wrote to me about an article she had been reading in a periodical concerning galaxies innumerable and the apparent limitlessness of space. She raised the following questions:

> If there is so much universe, can our wee earth be supremely significant and unique? Is man on earth *the* supreme creation or may there be more of him elsewhere, or other equally intelligent beings? If there are, has God revealed Himself to them as well as to us? If so, is the revelation that of an incarnation or has it taken some other form? Did we alone need and deserve a Christ? Has Christ gone from planet to planet revealing God? Can we alone claim Him? How do we widen our spiritual ideas to match our widening space concepts? Etc., etc., etc.!

Those are big and, for thoughtful people, inescapable questions. They are not wholly new questions. A psalmist in ancient Israel grappled with some of them: "When I consider thy heavens, the work of thy fingers, the moon and stars, which thou hast ordained; what is man, that thou art mindful of him? and the son of man, that thou visitest him?" Copernicus, the father of modern astronomy, grappled with more of them. His researches demonstrated that the planet we inhabit is not the center of the universe or the only stage on which the drama of the cosmos is being played out. Pascal wrote repeatedly of the universe encompassing and dwarfing him, as, for example, in the memorable passage: "When I consider the short duration of my life, swallowed up in the eternity before and after, the little space which I fill, and even can see, engulfed in the infinite immensity of spaces of which I am ignorant, I am frightened. Who has put me here? By whose order and direction have this place and time been allotted to me? The eternal silence of these infinite spaces frightens me. How many kingdoms know us not!" Part of the appeal of Pascal today is that he gives a voice to what we feel as we try to take in what science says about the awesome magnitude of the universe.

Our first reaction is that we and our beliefs are utterly insignificant and that all attempts to fathom the ultimate questions are futile. Life is shot through with mystery. As soon as we begin to touch the fringe of the infinite there is

> A deep beyond the deep,
> And a height beyond the height,
> And our hearing is not hearing,
> And our seeing is not sight.

About the beginnings of life, space, time, electricity, heat, Edison said: "We don't know the millionth part of 1 per cent about anything. We have a lot of hypotheses, but that is all." Our reaction may be even more negative. With our world like a microscopic speck of dust in a great star-city, with stars beyond number in the Milky Way and planets wheeling around them on which there may be life, we may doubt our own permanent significance, question whether we are the objects of the individual care of a benevolent Providence, resign ourselves to the conclusion that we are on our own, that the whole system of things about us is impersonal, neutral, heartless and godless. We may proceed on the assumption that the best we can do is learn to live by such intelligence as we can muster.

This, however, need not be our only or final reaction. Though, astronomically speaking, man is insignificant, the fact remains that man is the astronomer. His mind reaches out

into the immensities of the universe. The spirit within him
gives him a status and dignity that matter does not possess,
and frees him from astronomical intimidations. Watching an
eclipse, a scientist remarked, "When everything is said and
done, an ounce of brains is worth all that." As Pascal stated
the case: "Man is but a reed, the most feeble thing in nature;
but he is a thinking reed." He can make matter serve his purpose. He can beam his voice around the world in a dozen
languages. He can fly faster than sound. He has hands,
eyes, brains, and above all a heart with which he can give
back love for love. Physically, man is not impressive against
the universe; mentally, morally, spiritually, he is superior
to it.

Man's instinct is to go on to the limit of his creative capacities. He climbed trees and mountains to get up higher and
have a better view. Then he invented airplanes and balloons.
Now he is feverishly at work on rockets and satellites. The
extension of his control over nature is the basis of progress in
history. There are dangers in the process, the danger of Ti-
tanism, of pride of power, of abuse of power, of human presumption usurping the prerogatives of God, men storming
heaven itself, seeking to be masters of infinity. The times are
fraught with promise and peril. Twentieth-century man has
embarked on his greatest physical adventure—the exploration
of outer space, first interplanetary space, then interstellar
space, where the space sea drops sharply into almost unimag-
inable depths. The moon probes currently under way are an
infinitesimal attempt to measure the infinite. More and more
scientists have become convinced that there are numerous
planets resembling our own on which life has developed and
whose inhabitants are beings at least as intelligent as the human species of this earth. The possibility exists that signals
have been transmitted to us for many years from such planets,
and we have actually reached the stage where attempts are being made to tune in to any signals coming from more highly advanced beings than ourselves. To some this may seem fanciful
and fantastic, space fiction rather than sober fact. Scientific

research has frequently left the man on the street skeptical. When Stephenson's steam engine was first set on tracks the onlookers said, "It will never go, it will never go." Then as it got under way they exclaimed, "It will never stop, it will never stop!" Those who are incredulous about signals coming to us from other planets should note the statement of Harold C. Urey, Nobel prize winner: "In some other world that we know not of, other intelligent people are discussing the possibility of life on other planets. Contact with them would be the most magnificent thing one can imagine."

What does this mean for our Christian beliefs? Obviously, it means that we have got to do some fresh thinking. Religion should not be static while science is on the move. For one thing, *there must be an expansion of our convictions about man.* We who live on this planet still tend to think of ourselves as the center and crown of creation and the principal concern of Providence. We must become accustomed to the fact that we are peripheral, not central; that we are neither alone in the universe nor unique. If the scientific theorists are right, there are millions upon millions of other beings, not unlike ourselves, perhaps further advanced than ourselves. How does this affect the Christian doctrine of man—his origin, his nature, his final destiny? It is inconceivable that the truth about God, embodied and incarnate for us in Jesus Christ, is our sole possession to the exclusion of other possible beings elsewhere. If the other planets are inhabited, and by members of civilizations similar to ours, we who believe in the God and Father of our Lord Jesus Christ cannot but hold that He has revealed the same love and truth that we find in Christ to all, anywhere, who are able to receive them. God, we often affirm, has never left Himself at any time without a witness—at any time, and we now add, with a breathtaking awareness of its implications, in any place.

And if as a result of our probing into space an expansion of our convictions about man is imperative, even more so is *an expansion of our convictions about God.* He must be conceived as the Creator Sovereign not only of this earth but of

galaxies upon galaxies and worlds beyond worlds, of illimitable space and unmeasured time. This revives in sharper form
than ever before the question, "How can such a God be near to
mortals like ourselves or personally concerned about us?" The
answer is best sought along the line that quantitative standards of measurement are not ultimately as important as quali-
tative. What matters is the value of men and things, what they
are for rather than where they happen to be. On this view size,
space, time do not obscure but disclose the fullness of God's
purpose, the grandeur of His action, the constancy of His care
for all His creation. "There is no place where God is not." The
old affirmation has taken on fresh meaning. So also has the
opening clause of the Nicene Creed, "We believe in one God
the Father Almighty, Maker of heaven and earth, *and of all
things visible and invisible.*"

The majesty and mystery of the space revolution of today,
like the Copernican revolution of a bygone day, opens up to us
new vistas of God's power and a dazzling vision of His creation. "The undevout astronomer," it has been said, "is mad."
When we consider the heavens we stand in awe and reverence
before their Creator. We do not believe that they made themselves. They are the work of God's fingers. "The heavens de-
clare the glory of God." The immensities of the universe need
not frighten us. This is our Father's world. In our Father's
house are many mansions. And when Palomar telescope tells
us that there are far more mansions than we or our forebears
ever dreamed of, then what we are learning anew is that God
is infinitely greater and vaster than the mind of man can conceive. The starry spaces are tremendous but they are not
alien. We need not feel lost among the stars.

> In reason's ear they all rejoice,
> And utter forth a glorious voice;
> Forever singing as they shine,
> "The hand that made us is divine."

Where, in this context, is Christ relevant? Christians claim
that this is a "visited planet," that in Christ, God became man

for us and for our salvation. What about the other planets, and, if they are inhabited, what about the relation of those who inhabit them to Christ? Grounded in the Christian premise, the Christian doctrine of God, we can be confident that they have had bestowed on them the same love and grace we have known. The New Testament is emphatic that what God did in Christ, what He disclosed about Himself, what He revealed as the clue to life's meaning, has cosmic significance. Christ is not just incidental to human life, cut down in significance by the magnitude of the universe. The Divine Reality we meet in Him is basic to the whole structure of the universe, is in and behind and through everything everywhere as Origin and Agent and Goal. This belief is glowingly affirmed in the New Testament. "He is the image of the invisible God, the first-born of all creation; for in him all things were created, in heaven and on earth, visible and invisible, whether thrones or dominions or principalities or authorities—all things were created through him and for him. He is before all things, and in him all things hold together."

Something deeper than intellect is involved here. This is a judgment of faith, a value judgment. It is an intuitive certitude based on what we know of Christ and have experienced of His saving grace. We begin with the forgiveness of sins and end with a cosmology. At the heart of Christianity is the belief that "God so loved the world that he gave his only Son, that whoever believes in him should not perish but have eternal life." The same God must love all His other worlds also. In all this there is, of course, an element of necessary and profound inscrutability. Sir Isaac Newton said about his search for knowledge that he was like a child gathering a few shells on the shores of an illimitable ocean. If with our finite minds we could describe in detail, accurately and exhaustively, what God is doing with the universe, He would not be God. But it is our faith, inspired by Christ, that His nature is love and that His purpose for all that He has made is a purpose of love. For the rest, it behooves us to say what the Bible does: "O the depth of the riches both of the wisdom and knowledge of

God! how unsearchable are his judgments, and his ways past finding out! . . . For of him [He is the Source] and through him [He is the Agent] and to him [He is the Goal] are all things: to whom be glory for ever."

Part Two

TOWARD

A SUSTAINING FAITH

VIII

The Sin of Overwork

There is a story in the Old Testament about a man who had a prisoner entrusted to his charge and who was commanded to guard him with his life. For a while the man did just that, stood sentinel over the prisoner, did that and nothing else. But as the tide of battle moved in his direction, he thought he could do more by lending a hand with his sword. So he leaped into the fray, laid about him with a will—and came back to find that the prisoner had taken to his heels. When his superior officer demanded an explanation all that the man could stammer out was, "As thy servant was busy here and there, he was gone."

In the battle of life it is like that. Try to do two things at once and one of them may suffer. Try to do two things at once and the thing that suffers may be the thing of prior consequence to which you should be devoting yourself with undivided energy and attention. Every business executive can tell about able young men who fall down on the job because they do not concentrate on it; they have too many irons in the fire. People lose opportunities, not, as they sometimes complain, because opportunities never come their way, but because when the opportunities do come, they are not on hand to make the most of them. They are otherwise engaged, as a rule industriously engaged, but not on their real business. There was an old Puritan divine who wrote on the flyleaf of every book that came into his possession his name and under it: "Remember that thou art a Minister of the Word. Mind thy business."

That, however, is not my principal interest in this old story. What I want to emphasize is the phrase in the incident related above: "As thy servant was busy here and there." It accurately describes the character and conveys the tempo and atmosphere of modern living. Always on the move, operating on a tight and crowded schedule, keeping an anxious eye on the clock, engaged in an unending duel with time—this is life as millions know it. The pace is swifter, the pressure harder, the amount of work to be done heavier than they have any right to be.

We talk about sins of the body: gluttony and sensuality. We talk about sins of the disposition: bad temper, faultfinding, hypocrisy. Shouldn't something be said at some time or other about the sin of overwork? There are lots of people who never commit it, and give no impression of being tempted to commit it. They strike one as having a constitutional, even congenital, aversion not so much to hard work as to work of any kind. A man applied for employment in a department store and was told there was no opening for him. "You might find me a job of some kind," he replied. "All the work that I do will make no difference." Manifestly, I am not thinking, except by indirection, of such people. Nor am I addressing men and women for whom work is a drudgery, something from which to get away with all possible speed, who are yoked to an occupation which they do not love, for which they have no fitness, and in which consequently they are always more or less miserable. I am addressing myself rather to men and women whose friends say they haven't a lazy bone in their body, who love their work, believe in it, derive pleasure and satisfaction from it, but who are giving far too much time and strength and nervous energy to it, who are disregarding the strict limits—physical, mental, spiritual—which an individual may with impunity transgress. There are different degrees of sin and different kinds of sin. Isn't it high time more was said about the sin of overwork?

Of *over*work! Work itself is no sin. It has been spoken of as a punishment and a curse, yet it is far from being that. Dr. Samuel Johnson said that mankind was seldom more innocently employed than when engaged in its daily avocation. It was a characteristically sagacious remark, though it states the case too negatively. I much prefer Carlyle's repeated affirmation that a man perfects himself by working. "Blessed is the man who has found his work; let him ask no other blessing." To his hardworking mother Carlyle wrote about a certain Lady Sandwich: "Plenty of money, and fair health; but alas! *Nothing To Do*. That is not a very easy life after all." Work is one of our unchanging needs. Men tell themselves that when they retire they will have done with work, but unless they work at something they will go downhill incredibly fast. Work is the salt of life, preserving it from decay and corruption, giving it zest and relish. Henry van Dyke summed it up in the familiar lines:

> Let me but do my work from day to day
>> In field or forest, at the desk or loom,
>> In roaring market-place or tranquil room;
> Let me but find it in my heart to say,
> When vagrant wishes beckon me astray,
>> "This is my work; my blessing, not my doom;
>> Of all who live, I am the one by whom
> This work can best be done in the right way."
>
> Then shall I see it not too great, nor small,
>> To suit my spirit and to prove my powers;
>> Then shall I cheerful greet the labouring hours,
> And cheerful turn, when the long shadows fall
> At eventide, to play and love and rest,
> Because I know for me my work is best.

Work is not a sin, but overwork definitely is. There is what happens to the work itself. Industry knows that an over-wrought man is not going to turn out a good job. Labor suffers in quality when the laborer is kept too long on the stretch. The lesson is one that management itself is sometimes slow to learn. There are executives who are not turning in a first-class piece of work because they are so *"busy here and there."* As it is put in Yorkshire, they have "too much on their plate." At school or college did you ever have an exercise returned with the criticism, "This would have been better if more pains had been given to it"? It was not that you had been idle. The exercise did not have justice done to it because you had had too much to do. It is by concentration of energy rather than the dissipation of it that the best work is done. Unless you are a quite exceptional person, you can't do well, really well, more than a definite and limited amount of work. When a person overworks, the work itself suffers.

What is more, the worker suffers. Take what is liable to happen to his body. Let an individual go on from week to week and from month to month with every day planned and every hour filled, and what happens? Nature rebels. The body, under strain for so long, can take the strain no longer. It can stand only a certain amount of neglect and ill-treatment, and after that it revolts. Its vitality sapped, either it wears down or it breaks down.

Or, for constitutionally the body may be tough, consider what is liable to happen to the mind. The overworked person as often as not is irritable and nervous. His face tells eloquently what is happening inside him even if he does not. He can't relax. He feels the need of stimulants—cigarettes, coffee, cocktails—and more and more of them. He feels the need of tranquilizers. Finding that sleep is hard to come by, he learns to depend on sleeping pills. He is apt to flare up emotionally at the slightest pretext and in the most unreasonable and childish ways. In short, whether at home or business, he is not an easy person to live with. So life is sacrificed to the work of life. What should be made a means to an end becomes an end in itself. People become so occupied and preoccupied with their business that they practically sacrifice everything to it. It may be the health of their body or their mind. They may scarcely know their own children—at any rate, with any degree of understanding. They may give themselves no time to trim the lamp of friendship or to cultivate the life of their soul.

I make a plea for three things. The first of them is leisure. You owe it to yourself, your inner and deepest self, as well as to your relatives and associates, to slow up, moderate the pressure, take time out. There should be rhythms in human life, as there are rhythms in nature; first, stress of toil, and then happy release from it; first, diligent service, and then rewarding rest. "Never less idle than when idle" was the motto stitched by a Roman matron into her husband's dressing gown. It is pathetic when a man requires to have his eye everlastingly on the clock. We can't all live like Thoreau, but we can all learn from him. "My days," he said, "were not days of the week bearing the stamp of any heathen deity, nor were they minced into hours and fretted by the ticking of the clock." Make leisure. Insist on having it. It is one of the greatest of God's gifts and the best of medicines for body and soul. W. H. Davies never wrote a poem with more challenge in it for our hurrying, feverish age than when he composed the lines:

> What is this life if, full of care,
> We have no time to stand and stare.
>
> No time to stand beneath the boughs
> And stare as long as sheep or cows.
>
> No time to see, in broad daylight,
> Streams full of stars, like skies at night.
>
> .   .   .   .
>
> A poor life this if, full of care,
> We have no time to stand and stare.

I make a plea for a sense of perspective in the ordering of business and the management of time. Let us try to see things and to keep things in their true proportions. Work is important, but so is home and friendship and worship. A respectable citizen was in court the other day and saw his son sentenced to a term of imprisonment for a grave offense. The father made a plea for the boy. He had been allowed too much liberty and had been running wild. He, the father, had been out of the home day and night attending to his business. What do you suppose the judge told the father? "You have been too busy to do your duty."

There is something in that distressing incident for us all. Are we too busy to do our plain duty in the home, the church, the community? Are the prior claims receiving from us the consideration they merit? Are we so pushed and driven that some of the finest gifts of God to us—good books, inspiring music, the great world out-of-doors—go uncultivated? There are sins of the body, and they are bad. There are sins of the disposition, and they are worse. But what of this sin—so busy here and there, so occupied and preoccupied by this, that, and the other thing, that the things that matter most are crowded out. I recall something that was said by the late William Temple to a group of students at Oxford. He suggested that the world, as we live in it, is like a shop window into which some mischievous person has entered overnight and shifted all the price labels around so that the cheap things have the high-price labels on them and the really precious things are priced low. We let ourselves be taken in.

I am making a plea for leisure, for a sense of perspective, and third, for recognition of the supreme values for which Jesus stood. When a minister talks about the overcrowded life, and the pressure and the pace being greater than they should be, and the need for doing less and cutting things out and ensuring leisure, someone is certain afterward to remark, half in jest yet half in earnest, that he had better talk about something else or he may find himself faced with resignations from church committees and absences from the Sunday worship service. He has to take that risk. He knows from observation and experience what happens when some are told to slow down. The first activity to be affected is their religious activity. The first association to be curtailed is their church association. If they are to rest from their labors, Sunday morning seems to be the morning indicated.

That is why I am making a plea for recognition of the supreme values for which Christ stood. We have to practice discrimination. We have to pick and choose. Some things we should have no time for. Some things we must at all costs make time for. First things should be put first. The spiritual should have priority rights over the material. Our duty to God comes before our duty to anybody or anything else.

Jesus urged all this in His parable about the man who prepared a great feast and sent out invitations to his friends to be his guests. One by one they tendered apologies. The first had bought a farm and felt he must go and look it over. The second had made a deal that had brought him five yoke of oxen and he was on his way to try them. The third had recently married and could not attend. At that the host bade his servants go out and bring in to the feast the poor, the crippled, the blind. Do you see the point Jesus was making? All three men were engaged in perfectly legitimate activities, but they were so taken up with them, so engrossed and immersed in them, that they could find time for nothing else. They were oblivious to the other interests of life, to its higher interests; they allowed them to be crowded out.

That sort of thing still happens. If you are busy here and there, preoccupied by buying and selling, your days and your nights full, you are too absorbed in the world of sense to be intimately aware of the world of spirit. It may be that the word of God for you is this: Distinguish between what is primary and what is secondary, between what is urgent and what can wait, between what is of great value and what is of little consequence. Don't let yourself be taken in. Give the spiritual priority rights over the material. Put first things first. See that your duty to God comes before anybody or anything else.

IX

Why So Tense?

When I raise the question "Why so tense?" I am well aware that there are people who are never on the stretch either mentally or emotionally. They have an almost bovine placidity. Nothing seems deeply to disturb or concern them. On the eve of the French Revolution, Louis XVI presided at the opening of the States General. The Bishop of Nancy delivered an address in which he described the appalling condition of the French people. But the king fell fast asleep and the bishop's address was punctuated by the royal snores! There are conditions that ought to make for tension, that ought to rob us of peace of mind, that ought to alert and arouse us. Dives took Lazarus for granted. It is a question whether he even noticed him. At any rate, he ignored him. Jesus denounced with indignation such indifference and unconcern.

A thoughtful concern is one thing, however, and the perpetual anxiety that creates nervous tension another. I am thinking about men and women who are highly strung and nervously irritable. They find it difficult to relax. They are easily worked up into a fidgety and fretful state. They think more with their imagination than with their mind. They say things they regret as soon as the words are spoken. They try to cross bridges before they come to them. This sort of tension eats like acid into the soul. It does what hard work never does; it weakens and debilitates. Dean Inge defined worry as "the interest paid on trouble before it becomes due."

"The free man," Confucius told his disciples, "has no worries; the wise man no perplexities; the brave man has no fear." "But Master," one of them remarked, "you are describing yourself." At the opposite extreme are the folk I have in mind.

They are tense, edgy, strained. They have no center of peace in the midst of life's storms.

How do people get that way? It is the rush and pace, the pressure and problems of life. It is partly what we have described in the preceding chapter: the excessive demands made upon us by our work, or the hundred-and-one activities that eat into our lives, dissipating energy and vitality. It is what a city may do to us—the noise raucous and rasping, the crowds jamming their way into elevators and subways. It is the artificiality, the feeling that life is standardized, automatic, machine driven—like the device into which you put a coin in the penny arcade, gaze into a glass, move your head from side to side and look pleasant, then turn a handle and receive your portrait taken in a half-dozen different positions. It is the instinct to be somebody and to get somewhere and stay there. It is the hardness, the strident go-getting, the unabashed materialism, the fierce competition. On top of all this there is the general insecurity of the times: the scare headlines in the newspapers, the gloomy forebodings of radio commentators, the television screen which nowadays makes the international confusion vivid for us by bringing the principal actors in the drama right into our homes. The toll all this takes emotionally and mentally is heavy. To achieve inner serenity in the atomic age, or to maintain it against the assaults and invasions of a world as untranquil as ours, is not easy.

When we link the rush and pace of life with nervous tension, there is one fact we should take into account. We are concentrating overmuch on the physical levels of life. This is part of the reason for the sickness that is plaguing civilization. The concentration results in loss as well as gain. Our new laborsaving devices have made life easier, our machines have lessened toil. But if they have increased leisure they have also, paradoxically, increased the tempo of living. Life has been speeded up all around. We are in danger of being driven by the machines we have designed to serve us. A philosopher-statesman from India, after an extended visit to our country, offered this as a parting impression:

I think your young people should face frankly at the start of their career the basic fact that your business system is entirely dedicated to physical problems of making people comfortable, of feeding and clothing them, and of transporting them from place to place. The whole structure is founded on the surprising premise that the physical body is the first concern of society, collectively and individually. Physical welfare within certain limits is, of course, vital. But I believe that the civilized society of tomorrow will use 20% of its time in supplying physical needs instead of 75% to 90%, as you do in the United States.

It is an impression meriting consideration. If we spend so much time making a living that we have no time for, or no skill in, the business of making a life, if we concentrate on the body and neglect the spirit, we are certain to suffer from tension.

So much for diagnosis; what about prescription? What is the remedy for tension? Some time ago a popular magazine carried an article entitled "How to Get Rid of Tension." The directions were explicit. Readers were enjoined first to relax their muscles, second to breathe deeply and slowly, third to express courage and serenity outwardly, and they would then find their inward mood would come to correspond. The advice is good as far as it goes, but does it go far enough or deep enough? Here, too, the emphasis is mainly physical. Diet, reduce, keep yourself in trim, and all will be well. But is this always so? People suffering from a nervous breakdown will tell you, "I get no sympathy, for I look so well." A man can be, for a time, in pretty good shape physically, and yet nervously and emotionally be in deep trouble.

It sets one thinking about the characteristic emphases in the teaching of Jesus. He had a great deal to say about inward security, and He had the thing about which He talked. Outwardly, His was one of the most troublous lives that ever was lived. Think of the opposition He provoked, the antagonisms He aroused, the enemies He made. Think of the disappointments He suffered, the blows He sustained, the sorrows He endured. His life was not lived in a backwater but out on the ocean. There was tempest throughout His ministry, but there was a center of peace in the midst of the storms. At any time, by day or night, you might have gone to Him and found rest. He never had the haggard look of one whose resources were exhausted. He was free from the fretfulness and anxiety which weaken and debilitate so many of us.

What has He to say about being rid of tension? One characteristic emphasis is: Get your mind off yourself. So much of our tension, He tells us, is to be traced directly to self-preoccupation. If we could be rid of that, of self-consciousness, self-centeredness, self-seeking, we should, He says be less edgy and temperamental. We probably see this in the case of others, people who, if allowed, will talk all the time about themselves. Their attention is concentrated on their work, their worries, their petty achievements, their past experiences. They bore us, and what is equally serious, they bore themselves. That small, close house of self is not big enough for anybody—not airy and healthy enough for a spirit born to be free.

"Let a man deny himself"—that is the first demand Jesus makes of anyone who proposes to be His follower. It is a terribly difficult thing to do—to get oneself off the center of the stage, to have a frame of reference other than the first-person pronoun. How many of us succeed in the attempt, or persist with it? Let us frankly acknowledge what all experience attests as fact, that it somehow goes against the grain to put God where He should be—first—and others next, and self last. Yet in proportion as the thing is done, a blow is dealt at self-consciousness, self-centeredness, and self-interest, the roots of so much of our tension, and we are on the high road to serenity.

> If thou couldst empty all thy self of self,
> Like to a shell dishabited,
> Then might He find thee on the ocean shelf
> And say—"This is not dead,"—
> And fill thee with Himself instead.
>
> But thou art all replete with very *Thou*
> And hast such shrewd activity,
> That, when He comes, He says "This is enow

Unto itself—'Twere better let it be:
It is so small and full, there is no room for Me."

How are we to be rid of self? It will not be done in a day. It will not be done perfectly even in a lifetime. But just as we grow like those we live with, just as between husband and wife there sometimes develops an actual resemblance in features, so those into whose mind and heart the thought of Christ often comes as an inspiration and a standard for living grow like Him, even to the forgetting of self. They try to think of others in their joys and sorrows. They try to serve Christ in serving their fellows where and when and as they can. And the peace of God, which passes all understanding, garrisons their hearts and minds.

Another characteristic emphasis in the teaching of Jesus is: Don't be troubled about tomorrow; tomorrow will take care of itself. He doesn't mean that you are not to prepare for the emergencies of tomorrow; He means that you are not to work yourself up into a flurry and fever of apprehension when you get to thinking of all that you have to do tomorrow. Foresight is one thing, anxiety is another. Men and women become tired and run down not as a rule by what they are doing today but by their frightened concern over all they have to do tomorrow, and the day after tomorrow, and the day after that. I draw here on a personal experience. In 1946, when I was called to the Riverside Church, my mind was constantly preoccupied not by Riverside in 1946 but by Riverside in 1950, 1955, 1960. And it wasn't foresight, it was fretful, fidgety apprehension. I had to give it up. I had to school myself to rise each morning and thank God for the gift of one day, a new day, with a fresh opportunity of serving Him through serving Riverside. I had to remind myself that God didn't expect of me anything more than industry, fidelity, dedication, on a day-by-day basis. Foresight by all means, careful planning for the future, but no fretting and fussing over something that is in His hands, not mine.

So I say to you, thank God for the gift of today, and don't be scared about tomorrow and the day after tomorrow. Do

your best today; that is all God asks of you. Your part is to
carry out the task of today, and leave the rest to Him. Worry
has no driving power. It is like rust on the blade, like a brake
on the wheels. Since the future is out of your control, trust
God with it fully. Each morning you rise to a new page in the
book of your existence, on which you may write what you
please. You have the chance to work, to pray, to learn, to be
kind. Each morning God in His mercy lets you begin again.
Let hope come to you, as it ought to do, with God's new
bounty of a day. To all of us opportunity returns every morning. "So," says Jesus, "do not be troubled about tomorrow;
tomorrow will take care of itself."

But be sure you grasp what is back of that characteristic
emphasis. If you overlook it you will miss the shining secret
that makes it valid. All that Jesus says about living without
tension is grounded on belief in God. By all means relax your
muscles, breath deeply and slowly, but don't stop at that. Put
yourself in the way of the great healing and restoring energies of God. This is what our Lord kept urging again and
again. "Enter into your room and shut the door." "Pray to your
Father in secret." "Have faith in God." Put your confidence
in Him, the all-wise and loving Father. Believe that He cares
for you, and wills for you only the best. When you have done
all that you can, leave the results with Him. If you can accept
a truth because it comes from Christ, take that into your inner
life. It is not pious talk; first and last it is the secret of victorious living.

For many of us, life has lost strength and serenity because
in the ceaseless round of things, with all the tumult and pressure, we have lost touch with God. We are, as T. S. Eliot
phrased it, "hollow men," without real inwardness, without
invisible resources, the roots of our life not reaching down to
the eternal springs. We cannot become adequate to life in the
little noisy world of our own thoughts and plans. Our deepest
need is spiritual. Even the Master had to put Himself in the
way of the healing and restoring energies of God. He lived
in a hard world, among an oppressed people. His spiritual life

was greatly tried. He once thanked His disciples for standing by Him in His temptations. He had to have time for quiet and prayer, at the beginning of the day and at its end, and always He came out of the silence steady, strong, calm, able to say to harassed people, "My peace I give unto you." If He needed to slip away from the crowds and the bustle, if He needed a secret trysting place, if He had to make time for prayer, how much more do we!

A British newspaper carried a story some time ago about a farmer in South Africa. He had worked a small farm for thirty years, and had made little of it. One day he dug a bit deeper in his plowing, and discovered that underneath the shallow soil in which all his work had been done was a stratum of gold-bearing quartz. When the rock was exposed he found a reward that put all his former earnings in the shade. It is a parable of many lives. We spend ourselves on the surface of life, and with all our getting we may miss the things that matter most. Yet under the surface, in a deeper fellowship with God, there is the richest treasure of all: strength, serenity, zest for life, life filled with meaning and purpose.

There is in the Book of Job a sentence that sums it all up: "Acquaint now thyself with him, and be at peace."

X

Making Alibis Do Duty for Self-Blame

A college president has been telling how years of association with students have left him uncertain whether the degree
B.A. stands for Bachelor of Arts or Builder of Alibis. The remark reminds one of the story of the lad who went up from
his village to triumph in the university. He came back, alas,
without prizes, medals, or distinctions of any kind. At first
there was a little bewilderment. It gradually leaked out, however—he allowed it to leak out—that the professors had a spite
at him.

Students are not alone in making alibis do duty for honest
self-blame. Excuses, evasions, rationalizations are resorted to
by us all. They are handy and convenient devices and sooth-
ing to complacency and egoism. We can't bear to be put in
the wrong. We are on our feet in an instant protesting, explaining, rebutting. Judging by what psychologists tell us
about the defense mechanisms of the mind, the strongest motives determining behavior are not those which spring from
the impulses and instincts which we share with the animals,
such as hunger or self-preservation; they are those which
spring from the desire for self-vindication.

Reference has just been made to psychologists. People don't
always appreciate that some of the shrewdest and soundest
psychology is to be found in the Bible. It is a psychology pierc-
ingly true to life and, if you happen to be thinking of Freud
and Jung and Adler, extraordinarily up to date. Take the case
of Elijah and the sad sequel to the triumph on Mount Carmel.
The man who, singlehanded, fearlessly confronted the prophets of Baal, rose and ran for his life from the taunts and threats
of a woman. And when you track him down to his hiding place

in the wilderness what do you find him saying? Not, "I am a recreant, a coward, a poor apology for a prophet," but, "I, even I only, am left; and they seek my life, to take it away."

The defense mechanism is at work. He is making an alibi do duty for self-blame. You couldn't find a clearer example of what psychologists mean by *rationalization*. His mind has arrived at a compromise which will give it a measure of peace. He is not deliberately manufacturing an excuse to save his feelings. You can't charge him with conscious hypocrisy. He is evading the facts, but he is unconscious of evading them. This is what makes rationalization so mischievous. Elijah is emphasizing a fact—his solitariness in Israel—which, while it is true as far as it goes, is irrelevant. It is obscuring the redundant fact, that he has shirked his duty, deserted his post, been frightened out of his wits by Jezebel.

In the New Testament there is a case of a slightly different sort. Judas grumbled volubly when Mary broke the alabaster box of perfume and poured it over the feet of the Savior. The perfume, he complained, might have been sold for three hundred pence, to be given to the poor. Judas was rationalizing. His estimate of the cost of the perfume was probably quite accurate, but the reference to the poor was a defense mechanism of his mind. It covered up the greed which prevented him from seeing any purpose or beauty in what he called "this waste." I don't know that we can charge him any more than Elijah with conscious hypocrisy. He was evading the ugly facts about himself, but he may have been unaware that he was evading them.

What we call our conscious mind is only a small part of our total mind. The illustration generally employed to picture the structure of the mind is that of an iceberg floating in the ocean; one-ninth of it visible above the surface, eight-ninths hidden below. Underneath self-conscious processes of thought and will are unconscious processes, obscurely motivated passions, impulses, prejudices, illusions and delusions, likes and dislikes. It isn't a simple matter for any of us to put a finger on the ugly facts about ourselves. They slip so easily into the unconscious. We are such born rationalizers. A Sunday School teacher told Dr. Bernard Hart that he had become an atheist. He was able to advance a reasoned case for his atheism. He was genuinely of the opinion that his denial of belief in God was intellectually grounded. It was not. Like a great deal of atheism, it was emotionally grounded. A few talks with Dr. Hart brought out that the girl to whom the Sunday School teacher was engaged had eloped with a fellow Sunday School teacher. That was what accounted for the atheism. The reasoned argument in its support was an unconscious rationalization, a false reason because the true one was repugnant and would have dealt a blow to his self-esteem.

We all make alibis do duty for self-blame. When we make a mistake, it is a slip; when somebody else makes it, it is a blunder. What in us is righteous indignation, in another is bad temper. What for us is a clever stroke of business, in a fellow competitor is unethical behavior. A man tells himself that he is merely indulging in a harmless flirtation; or a woman, that romance and love have at last come into her life. They are rationalizing, dressing up reprehensible conduct in an idealistic light, turning a blind eye on an indefensible course of action, persuading themselves that they are actuated by worthy motives. The words with which they should be facing their consciences are nasty words, nasty words because they stand for nasty things, words like fornication and adultery.

There is another defense mechanism of the mind which psychologists call *projection*. The word, like the science of psychology, may be modern, but the thing is as ancient as the hills. And once again, if you want a crystal-clear illustration of what is meant by projection, you cannot do better than turn to that supreme psychological textbook and source book, the Bible. After David had done a very contemptible thing in the matter of the wife of Uriah, the Hittite—not only taken Bathsheba from Uriah but put him in the front line of battle so that he was killed—the prophet Nathan came and told him the story of the rich man with many flocks and herds who took the poor man's one ewe lamb. David was passionately indignant with the rich man, condemned him to death there and then. It never occurred to him, until Nathan courageously declared *"Thou* art the man," that the story was an exact picture of his own conduct. He had repressed the memory of it and the guilt of it—memory and guilt alike had sunk into his unconscious where they were not dead and buried but festering and ulcerating—and he gained a measure of relief, as we all do, by projection, by being angry with his own fault when he saw it in someone else.

What a defense mechanism—condemning in others what we are guilty of ourselves but refuse to admit! Here, beginning with preachers, is how J. A. Hadfield, Harley Street specialist, states the case.

It is a well known fact that preachers are always preaching against the sins to which they are, unconsciously, most prone (and usually rigidly avoid those to which they are consciously addicted). It is literally true that in judging others we trumpet abroad our secret faults. We personalize our unrecognized failings, and hate in others the very faults to which we are secretly addicted. We are annoyed with the incompetence of others only because we refuse to admit our own real incompetence. Most of our emotions are directed against ourselves. We are intolerant of the lazy, slovenly, "footling" ways of others because this tendency is a constant temptation to us. We condemn bigotry, meanness, or cynicism in others because we are potential bigots, misers and cynics. We cannot bear conceited people because we are conceited without knowing it. Paul breathed out threatenings and slaughter against the Christians probably because he was three parts a Christian. . . . On the other hand, an easygoing tolerant spirit is often merely the projection of our tolerant attitude toward our own hidden sins. We forgive in others what we desire to forgive in ourselves, for by so doing we temper the sting of self-condemnation. Allow any man to give free vent to his feelings about others and then you may with perfect safety turn and say, "Thou art the man!"

What is behind all this defense mechanism, this building of alibis? Ugly facts we will not acknowledge and of which we may not even be conscious. Cowardice in the case of Elijah. Greed in the case of Judas. Adultery and murder in the case of David. People repress into their unconscious, desires, impulses, feelings which they refuse to acknowledge because the acknowledgment would be distasteful and a blow to their self-esteem. Just as we dissociate ourselves from those who have insulted us, so we refuse to recognize or identify ourselves with our faults and weaknesses. This is how unethical behavior, immoral conduct, censoriousness, selfishness and pride become dissociated; we are practically unaware of their existence. If two people have a quarrel, and come separately to tell you about it, you will often notice that their respective accounts of what happened differ, sometimes to a surprising extent. This is not because one of them is telling lies, or both of them, but because they each repress, and therefore fail to remember or recognize the weak points in their own case. There is a story of a Carthusian monk who was explaining to a stranger the strong points of his little-known Order. "As for learning, we are not to be compared to the Jesuits," he said. "When it comes to good works, we don't match the Franciscans. As to preaching, we are not in a class with the Dominicans. But," he concluded, "when it comes to humility, we're tops." Behind all defense mechanisms of the mind are ugly facts which we will not acknowledge and of which we may not even be conscious.

Why are ugly facts kept out of our consciousness? Because we need to stand well in our own eyes. We can't afford to forfeit self-respect; when that goes, practically everything goes. It has been said that to have good foreign relations with others we must have good domestic relations with ourselves. Contempt from those about us is hard to bear, but may God pity the wretch who has contempt for himself. We go to almost any length to preserve a certain kind of self-respect—projection, fantasy, compensation, rationalization, repression, one defense mechanism after another. And all because we cannot endure to be put in the wrong. We have to find some way of assuring ourselves that we are all right, some way of holding our heads up, facing the world. Without some sort of self-acceptance, there is nothing for it but suicide. We must be at rights with ourselves, even if it means making wrong seem right.

But to make wrong seem right, to ignore, repress, and forget it, is not to dispose of it. Down it goes into the unconscious, and what mischief it works there, festering, suppurating, ulcerating. For the unconscious is not a storehouse but a mill. Guilt feelings are not disposed of when they are disguised; they are only covered up. They are not dead and buried. Though underground, they are very much alive; that is demonstrated by the fashion in which a sentence in a sermon or a novel, a scene in a film or a play, or a chance meeting will bring them right up from the unconscious to the conscious level of the mind. Much of the hypertension, neurasthenia, and neurosis of our time comes from the failure of people to live with themselves, to adapt not only to their environment but to themselves. We have to be at rights with ourselves, but the only way to be that is to face the facts about ourselves. If you have a bad temper, don't disguise the fact, acknowledge it. If you have strong sex urges, don't turn a blind eye on them, recognize them for what they are. There was the man who looked at himself in a mirror for some minutes, and then said out loud, "You dirty cad." And after that he went out and began life over again. To live happily with yourself you have to be honest with yourself. Alibis, evasions, rationalizations—they are all mischief-makers. Think of what the Bible has to say about that. Think of Jacob at Peniel. He had deceived his father Isaac, his brother Esau, his uncle Laban, and as a result of crafty dealing was a prosperous man. But just like J. P. Marquand's Willis Wayde, he had never stopped long enough to take a good look at himself. He had been running away from himself for a long time. At Peniel he had it out with himself. "What kind of a man am I? What is my real character?" He wrestled all night, not only with God but with something demonic in himself, and after a long struggle he got down to rock bottom. "I am Jacob—a twister." And it was then, evasions done with, disguises cast aside, that he became a new man, no more Jacob but Israel—a prince with God.

The same miracle of transformation took place in the Prodigal Son. It was when he was honest with himself with a frank and merciless honesty, and said, "I have sinned," that he came to his true self. A new chapter of his life began that very day. A new chapter can begin for you if, bidding good-by to self-excuse, self-pity, self-defense, you will face the facts about yourself, get right down to them instead of running away from them, if you will say to yourself, "Yes, that is the kind of person I am, that is the sort of thing I am capable of doing and have done, but, by the grace of God, I can be different, and will be." Robert Wicks, who was chaplain of Princeton University for many years, said, out of his long experience with students, that whenever a boy turned about-face and settled down to a worth-while life, the boy always traced the change back to some experience that made him look at himself until he was ashamed of himself; out of recognition and repentance came the resolve to do and be better.

All through this chapter I have been drawing on the psychological insights of the Bible. There is one thing the Bible keeps saying that some psychologists and psychiatrists never say: To be right with yourself get closer to God. No sooner had the Prodigal acknowledged "I have sinned" than he made the resolve "I will arise and go to my father." This is what Jesus urges on us. When we see ourselves for what we really are, are ashamed of ourselves, have difficulty in accepting ourselves, we can be sure of one thing—God will accept us. About nothing else is Jesus more emphatic. There is One who can deliver us from self-pity, self-excuse, self-defense. Though we are tied and bound with the chains of our sins, yet in His great mercy He can loose us from our chains, can empower us to live nobly and courageously. He believes in us, sees beneath our worst to our best, helps us to believe in ourselves because of His faith in us, calls forth what is fine and splendid in us, quickens our hope, revives our faith, helps us to begin life anew. In the presence of God our littleness is apparent, but His is not the greatness that creates a sense of inferiority. It humbles, and yet it exalts. It challenges, inspires, energizes. Nothing produces a greater happiness. Nothing gives such a sense of well-being. Nothing brings a deeper peace. I can say nothing more important to you than the thing our Lord said again and again: "Get closer to God." For there is the ultimate secret—not what you can do to justify yourself but what God can do for you by making His strength your own.

XI

The Conflict of Loyalties

Loyalty is one of the royal virtues. He who is without it lacks a quality indispensable to true character. It is not just a personal quality. It is the cement of society. In every realm—the home, the church, the nation, the community of nations—loyalty is what holds human life together, gives it cohesiveness and solidarity. Without it all these institutions would fall apart.

The problem for many, however, is not how to be loyal—faithful to love, to duty, to vows, to obligations—but how to deal with conflicting loyalties. Naaman, the Syrian, cleansed of his leprosy, swore that he would thenceforth be loyal to the God of Israel, but he had hardly done so before he realized that when he went back to Syria he would have to go with his master in the line of duty into the temple of Rimmon, and when his master bowed down to worship Rimmon, he would be expected to do likewise. One can sympathize with Naaman's dilemma. There was the duty he owed to the God of Israel and the duty he owed to his monarch, the king of Syria. "Bowing down in the house of Rimmon," has become a proverbial expression to denote the danger and dishonesty associated with compromise. Yet when loyalties conflict, how is compromise to be avoided?

It may be a conflict of loyalties in the course of the day's business. An employee is asked to do something that his conscience does not approve. Dependent on him and his earnings are his wife and children. What is he to do? Register a protest? Give up the job? Tell himself that the employer is responsible, not the employee? In 1742, John Woolman, the Quaker, was a clerk. He kept a journal and in it set down this entry.

My employer, having a Negro woman, sold her, and desired me to write a bill of sale, the man being waiting who bought her. The thing was sudden; and though I felt uneasy at the thought of writing an instrument of slavery for one of my fellow-creatures, yet I remembered that I was hired by the year, that it was my master who directed me to do it, and that it was an elderly man, a member of our Society, who bought her; so through weakness I gave way and wrote it; but at the executing of it I was so afflicted in my mind, that I said before my master and the friend that I believed slave-keeping to be a practice inconsistent with the Christian religion. This, in some degree, abated my uneasiness; yet as often as I reflected seriously upon it I thought I should have been clearer if I had desired to be excused from it, as a thing against my conscience; for such it was.

The conflict of loyalties may take place in wartime. In 1941, when I was teaching at McMaster University in Hamilton, Ontario, a student came to talk with me. He told me that he hated war and that, as a Christian, he didn't think he should have any part in it. But he loved Canada, and he felt that the whole democratic way of life was in mortal danger. Besides, he said, he couldn't endure to see so many of his classmates go off into the service while he stayed at home and, in comfort and security, made a study of philosophy and ethics. Well, he enlisted in the Royal Canadian Air Force, got his wings, was shot down over the Irish Sea, was the last man (his comrades testified) to bail out, and he alone of the crew was never seen again. Stanley Gaudin, a fine upstanding lad, the only son of a widowed mother—I can see him yet as he discussed with me the problem of conflicting loyalties.

What a fierce and terrible conflict it is! There was the Christian member of the French Resistance Movement who wrote as he went underground:

I ask God that He now forgive my sins, and the decision which I voluntarily take this day (for I know that recourse to violence has need of pardon). But I am leaving without hate and fully convinced that we Christians have not the right to leave it to non-Christians alone to offer their lives.

If only all that was asked were to offer one's life! Did that French Christian have to do what so many in the Resistance felt obliged to do—forge ration books, steal passports, liquidate traitors, come stealthily on an enemy from behind and knife him? There was a scene in the film *The Cruel Sea* in which the captain exclaimed in anguish of mind after sinking a U-boat at the cost of dropping a depth charge among his own men struggling in oily waters: "I suppose you must just go on and do what you have to do—and say your prayers."

Consider the conflict of loyalties to which thousands upon thousands of our fellow Christians on the other side of the Iron Curtain are being subjected right now. The issue of loyalty to one's country and government poses one of the most poignant and difficult questions in life. What does a Christian in one of the satellite countries feel about it all? For example, what should be the attitude of a Christian when he sees a government in power that denies the spiritual basis upon which he himself interprets life, but at the same time is carrying through land reforms which, as a Christian, he has long desired to see? We ought not too quickly to come up with dogmatic answers to those pressing questions. We are not living on the spot. We are not familiar with all that is at stake. We do not know at first hand the tension that such conflicting loyalties create, nor are we having to work out the problem as they have to in concrete situations and personal relationships.

Thus far I have been doing no more than stating the case, showing how a conflict of loyalties may arise in the course of the day's business, in wartime, in a Christian's relation to his country or his government when violence is done to Christian principles. Even so, just to state the problem is to render a service. These are issues about which we should be sensitive and to which we should give careful thought. It is easier, of course, to pose the problem than to come up with solutions. There are no simple solutions. It is hard to be a Christian.

For instance, when should one obey, and when defy, a law which one on soul and conscience believes to be unwise or even morally wrong? It is easy to say that the voice of conscience should be supreme. But is there no difference between an instructed and an uninstructed conscience? It is easy to say that no man-made law should override the dictates of conscience. But some deference is due to established authority. How and where should the line be drawn?

Is it ever right to tell a lie? Even as I raise the question, I think of Carlyle's thundering reply: "Truth! though the heavens crush me for following. No Falsehood! though a whole celestial lubberland were the price of apostasy." But I think, too, of the saintly bishop in Victor Hugo's great novel coolly fabricating a lie to save a thief from arrest, and saying to him: "Jean Valjean, my brother, you belong no longer to evil, but to good. It is your soul I am buying for you. I withdraw it from dark thoughts and from the spirit of perdition and I give it to God." For the bishop, the virtue of truth was related to justice and mercy. Facts, he saw, could actually get in the way of truth. If you pass judgment not on the bishop's action but on his motives, you will let him go uncondemned.

Is it possible to do always what is ideally right? Stanley Gaudin, the Canadian student to whom I referred earlier, did not find it possible. And many another has found himself in a position where, through no fault of his own, there seemed no right course open to him but only a choice between evils. That was what going to war meant in the forties for countless young Americans, not a holy crusade but the lesser of two evils. So, rather than take his country into war Neville Chamberlain tried appeasement for the sake of keeping the peace. It was a compromise—and there is rarely anything idealistic about a compromise. You probably criticize him. So do I. After the event we can all do that. Yet Chamberlain, born and bred in Unitarianism, was probably no lover of compromise. A policy of appeasement is not heroic. Take the case of Hans Simons, former president of the New School for Social Research. Living in Hitler's Germany, the conflict he was torn by was between compromising for self-preservation or becoming a martyr for a cause. He was in a position where he had the choice of either challenging National Socialism openly, or compromising to the extent of saving his own life. In the first case, he reasoned, he would have ended up in a concentration camp and been silenced. In the other, he could hold his tongue for the time being and try to get out, and from the outside fight National Socialism. He recognized that there were strong arguments either way. He says that nobody who has not had to make them for himself can possibly know how irreconcilable they are. Repeatedly in life it is like that—the choice not between black and white but between differing shades of gray.

A Christian, however, will not make this an excuse for lowering his standards and conforming to the ways of the world. He will not give up trying to apply his Christianity to everyday life. He will strive to act as nobly as possible in every situation, in wartime, in race relations, in the fiercely competitive world of business, seeking always to select the better of two alternatives. By so doing, he will not only cultivate a worthy character but will do his part in building up a better state of society in the future, so that things impossible for him may be possible for future generations.

Maxims like "One step at a time" and "Half a loaf of bread is better than none" are not necessarily maxims of worldly prudence. Those who by nature are idealistic have no patience with them, are contemptuous of them. But doesn't it often happen that the idealist, after declaiming indignantly about an evil situation, withdraws into an ivory tower? Two global wars and the present state of the world ought to have taught us that the human conditions for an ideal solution of our national and international problems are not yet present. As Christians we shall serve our generation most by seizing on whatever of good the situation of the moment makes possible. By the vigilant detection and the practical use of each concrete opportunity of improvement and reform we can lift society to a higher level.

I know of no Christian of our time who was more concerned to apply his Christianity to everyday life, to business, to politics, to questions of war and peace, to national and international relations, than William Temple. But if he had his head in the air he kept his feet on the ground. He was a practical Christian statesman. He believed that Christian principles would be workable if a sufficient number of people would get behind them, but he accepted the fact that people by and large don't get behind them, and he joined hands with them to secure the lesser good they were willing to support. He worked with his fellows for the second best when they were not ready to work for the best. He preferred to achieve in co-operation with them an attainable good, while at the same time he kept pointing them to the supreme good. He once said, "It is certainly a mistake to begin with the picture of a supposedly ideal system and try to establish it. The way of Christian progress is to ask where an existing system is break-ing down and readjust it in the light of Christian principles." If this be compromise, it is, as with the bishop in Victor Hugo's novel, a compromise of action, not of ideals.

Even so, compromise has its limits. What those limits are each of us must find out in each case for himself, keeping be-fore us continually the example and spirit of Christ. We shall be on our guard, prayerfully and constantly, against a lower-ing of standards and a cowardly compliance with the de-mands of self-interest and worldliness. We shall be on our guard, prayerfully and constantly, lest a minor loyalty lead us to sacrifice a major one. That is the thing especially to avoid: a little loyalty to one's family, one's profession, one's class, one's race, pressed at the expense of a larger one. Jesus has so much to say about that. Devoted to our family, but uncon-cerned about other families. Devoted to our nation, but caring little about other nations. Devoted to our denomination, but isolated from, if not critical of, our brethren in other denom-inations.

And first, last, always, we must remember that our supreme loyalty is to God. John Gunther tells us that whenever he visits a country and asks about the leading political personality and talks to him, he tries to focus on two questions: "What are the real sources of power behind the man? What does he believe in most?"

What do you and I believe in most? When the choice of loyalties finally narrows down, in what direction does it point? For that is the real source of power behind us. Is it our family? Is it our profession? Is it our nation? Is it God?

And now, as an illustration of the way in which a Christian can deal with the conflict of loyalties, I quote the tribute of a friend to Judge Augustus N. Hand.

Those who watched the victory of the spirit in Judge Hand gained new insight and new courage. They became convinced that beyond the clash of interests and the compromise of competing claims there can be found standards of rectitude and generosity, and that in the search for these standards and in the steadfast adherence to them lies the triumph of man. To quote the words that the poet Archibald MacLeish wrote in his honor, Judge Hand taught us that—

> We are neither weak nor few.
> As long as one man does what one can do—
> As long as one man in the sun alone
> Walks between the silence and the stone
> And honors manhood in his flesh, his bone,
> We are not yet too weak, nor yet too few.

XII

On Wanting to be Liked

C. S. Lewis says about a character in one of his novels: "Mark liked to be liked. There was a good deal of the spaniel in him." Isn't there, for that matter, a good deal of the spaniel in all of us? Nothing runs deeper in human nature than the desire to be appreciated. You see it in small children: the craving for approval, the attempt to secure attention and recognition, the courting of the limelight. You see it in teenagers: physically awkward and self-conscious, often emotionally insecure, eager to be acceptable and congenial in their circle, dreading the possibility of going friendless. You see it in people of every age: the desire to be a success socially, to be wanted, welcomed, esteemed, not to be left out of things.

Nobody who saw Arthur Miller's play, *Death of a Salesman*, will readily forget Willy Loman, its central character. Perhaps the majority of those who saw the play discovered at some time in the evening that they were identifying themselves with Willy, for while in many respects he was an abnormal character, in one respect he reflected a widespread tendency. He wanted to be well liked. He put great emphasis on social acceptance. For him, social acceptance was the guarantee of financial success as well as of prestige. To his sons he said:

I thank Almighty God you're both built like Adonises. Because the man who makes an appearance in the business world, the man who creates a personal interest, is the man who gets ahead. Be liked and you will never want. You take me, for instance. I never have to wait in line to see a buyer. "Willy Loman is here!" That's all they have to know, and I go right through.

84

There is a moral issue at stake in all this, and not a minor but a major one. Underneath Willy Loman's desire to be well liked there was a fierce competitiveness. What he was really after was "to come out number one," and it was what he most wanted for his sons. Nearly every normal person wants to be liked, wants approval, acceptance, recognition. There is nothing wrong in itself with that. It is natural to prefer commendation to criticism, and popularity to ostracism. The second clause of the commandment which Jesus made basic and fundamental, on which as He put it "depend all the law and the prophets" reads, "You shall love your neighbor *as yourself.*" There is a place for a proper self-esteem, and this of necessity involves being in happy, harmonious relations with others. The two—liking oneself and being liked—are inextricably bound up with each other. The irrational hostility that people vent on one another is often projected self-hate. In the days before his conversion, Tolstoi wrote in his diary, "It is myself I am weary of and find intolerable and a torment. I want to fall asleep and forget myself and cannot." Feeling like that about himself, Tolstoi must have been a sore trial to his relatives and associates. To live with himself, a person has in some degree to like himself and to be liked by others.

This is where, for numbers of people, practical difficulties arise. If because of some defect, poor appearance, or lack of the social graces, if because of problems of personality and temperament, if through the neglect or lovelessness of others they are disliked, unwanted, unpopular, they are certain to be unhappy. There was once a man who was wealthy, prominent, successful in business, yet with angularities of character that made for antipathy and hostility in practically all his social contacts. He knew that people were not drawn to him, were not fond of him, and while he gave every impression of being a self-sufficient person he was secretly and bitterly frustrated. A pampered little Pekingese dog was shrewd enough to get around him, and he would indulge it with salted almonds. "Believe the little beast likes me," he told an acquaintance. "He's always looking at me." It was cupboard love, but

it gave him the sensation which of all others he most lacked—
that of being liked for his own sake. Pathetic, is it not? And
the story is one that we can parallel from our own observation.
If we knew all the attending circumstances in such cases, we
would be much more compassionate than we ordinarily are.
Criticism of such people is like striking a wounded animal
desperately in need of solicitous care. They want to love and
to be loved, but they don't know how to do the one or to win
the other. The danger is that in their attitude to life and people they may become cold and hard, an attitude that in turn
only further isolates them from their fellows.

Consider to what lengths people will go to be liked. Some
will behave like a spaniel, will fawn on those whose friendship or favor they covet, will shower praise or attention on
them to ingratiate themselves, will be docile, obsequious, ser-
vile. Polonius, as Shakespeare depicts him, was just such a
person.

HAMLET:	Do you see yonder cloud that's almost in shape of a camel?
POLONIUS:	By th' mass, and 'tis like a camel indeed.
HAMLET:	Methinks it is like a weasel.
POLONIUS:	It is back'd like a weasel.
HAMLET:	Or like a whale.
POLONIUS:	Very like a whale.

And, on the other hand, some, because of the craving for appreciation, will accept fawning and flattery, detecting neither
its absurdity nor the insincerity back of it. Wordsworth,
praised effusively to his face by a disciple from Scotland, was
heard remarking a few minutes later that the Scot was the
most intelligent and well-informed Scot he had ever met!

Worse than this is the fact that to be liked, to secure social
acceptance, people will compromise with principle. They conform to subtle but strong group pressures. They allow themselves to be persuaded that in adhering to certain convictions
and standards they are not being courageous but are just stub-
born. Young people who have no inclination to drink hard

liquor or to adopt a free and easy attitude in the matter of sex begin to feel that abstinence on their part will be construed as a criticism and condemnation of those who are unhampered by inhibitions on either score. President John Kennedy said that when he entered Congress he was told, "The way to get along is to go along." His comment in that connection merits quotation.

Perhaps if the American people more fully comprehended the terrible pressures which discourage acts of political courage, which drive a Senator to abandon or subdue his conscience, then they might be less critical of those who take the easier road—and more appreciative of those still able to follow the path of courage. . . . Americans want to be liked—and Senators are no exception. . . . We enjoy the comradeship and approval of our friends and colleagues. We prefer praise to abuse, popularity to contempt. Realizing that the path of the conscientious insurgent most frequently is a lonely one, we are anxious to get along with our fellow legislators, our fellow members of the club, to abide by the clubhouse rules and patterns, not to pursue a unique and independent course which would embarrass or irritate the other members.

So, "the way to get along is to go along." What the late President is saying—it is the thesis of his book, *Profiles in Courage* —is that it takes stamina to adhere to principles, to keep one's standards, to be ready if need be on their account to face criticism, ridicule, ostracism, impoverishment.

Look now at another aspect of the case—the things people will do when they are not liked, when they are unwanted and lonely. The positive course would be to try to find out what is wrong, what the defects of temperament or character are, or what the quirks of personality are that make for unpopularity. As a rule, however, we are unconscious of such defects. On the side of our shortcomings and limitations we do not see ourselves as clearly as we see our neighbors. If we are vain or petty or priggish or dogmatic, we are usually the last to realize it. The sharp critic, the gossip, the bore, the prima donna are often unaware why people cold-shoulder them. Being cold-shouldered they frequently reimburse themselves by a double dose of self-esteem. Dr. J. A. Hadfield had a patient who told him she was overwhelmed by a feeling of not being wanted. He found that she had a fantasy of herself as "such a sweet delicate little thing, with so lovable a disposition," and wondered how anybody could not help loving her. Yet the fact was only too obvious that many managed not to like her, and because *everybody* did not love her, she complained that *nobody* loved her. Vanity run to seed is not a pretty sight, and in itself it accounts for much unpopularity.

It may work the other way. Those who are unsought, shunned, avoided, made to feel of no account, are as likely to give way to self-depreciation as they are to reimburse themselves by a double dose of self-esteem. Unlike those described in an earlier chapter, some are driven to extravagant self-blame rather than alibis. Minor criticism may foster major depression. A student, depressed by his low grades and his failure to qualify for admission to a fraternity, exclaimed abjectly, "I can't do anything right." An adolescent girl, no plainer than the average, turned from her mirror crying, "I'm so ugly! I'm so gosh awful *ugly!*" Anyone who works with people knows how common it is for folk of every age to have disparaging feelings about themselves, and the more so if they have come in any sense to think of themselves as outsiders. Not being liked by others, they cease to like themselves. They are plagued by a sense of inferiority. They attribute graces and abilities to other people, graces and abilities which, if they only knew it, the others do not possess; and they yearn to be like them, to think, speak, act as they do, and sometimes they take to aping them. An infinite amount of tragedy comes from this inner self-contempt.

What we all need—for there is something for all of us here—is to face the facts about ourselves, what we are and what we can and cannot do. We do not have to hide our inadequacies or build up our capacities unrealistically. God does not ask any of us to do more than be ourselves, our real, true, best selves. Jesus, it should be remembered, reverenced men and women, and insisted that they should reverence themselves.

"You shall love your neighbor as yourself"; He made that a great, guiding principle. We are to be self-respecting individuals. Thank God for your individuality, for your gifts whether small or great. Try to realize your value to God and to your fellows. Remember that when God made you, He broke the mold.

Who are the people who are liked, really liked? Dale Carnegie's book notwithstanding, they are not the persons who deliberately set out to win friends and influence people. A woman is never further from charming than when she seeks to charm. A contrived popularity is as shoddy as it is superficial. In most circles there are individuals who maneuver themselves into the limelight and invite attention. They are facile in speech, witty in repartee, always able to match a good story with a better one. Yet with all their brilliance, we do not like exhibitionists. They too closely resemble hucksters pushing their wares on us. Dorothy Day in her autobiography says about one of her friends, "Perhaps she was loved because she was so unselfconscious, so interested in others, so ready to hear and discuss all that interested them." That seems to me to cut deep. The people who are really liked get beyond self through love. They are interested in people; they treat all whom they meet with chivalry and courtesy; they are quick to appreciate and encourage. What attracts us to them is their unselfconsciousness. They are as natural, as artless, as humble as lovely flowers.

Nothing runs deeper in human life than the hunger for appreciation. We never outgrow the need for an approval that will make our efforts seem worthwhile. Interest and encouragement, particularly in the small-change of life, are as essential for the health of the mind and spirit as food and drink, fresh air and sunshine and occasional holidays, are necessary for the health of the body. In some quarters there is a curious impression that to praise a person is to make him conceited. Almost without exception, the reverse is the case. Appreciation induces humility. There are few things so humbling as warm-hearted recognition and approval. The recipient feels unworthy of what is said but is desirous of making it true. It is the minor tragedy of many lives that people, week in and week out, go on and on, and hardly anybody ever utters a word of praise of them or of their efforts.

Let no one think that all this is remote from religion. In point of fact it is close to the beating heart of all true religion. At any rate, Jesus put unvarying emphasis on it. He showed unfailing interest in people. He treated them always with chivalry and courtesy. He was a great encourager, never sparing in commendation. It was a habit with Him to see first in man, woman, and child what was likeable, not what was blameworthy. He went about looking for the good in people, and finding it in marvelous ways and in unexpected quarters. He saw in shifty, unstable, unreliable Simon a man capable of becoming solid and dependable as granite rock. He saw in the greedy little quisling, Zacchaeus, the possibilities of a great and generous life. He saw in Mary Magdalene a woman not yet beyond redemption's point. It was because Jesus enabled men to see what was best in themselves that He did them so much good. Those who make us feel hopeless or useless or wicked do not render us a service. If only they knew it, they merely confirm us in our own discouraged opinion of ourselves. But those who like us can get anything out of us.

There lay Christ's power. Unprincipled men, and light, flippant women felt constrained to say about Him: "This man likes us, sees something redeemable in us, does not treat us as the flotsam and jetsam of humanity." *He liked them into liking themselves.* It was thus that they won their way to a new self-respect, which again and again was the origin, as it was the basis, of their recovery and transformation.

Consider the experience of the first disciples. "Follow Me," Christ told them, "and I will make you fishers of men." He did make them. Who could have foretold that they would initiate a movement that would leave its mark indelibly on the world? But Christ looked past their limitations, saw beneath the unpromising exterior, discerned in them fitness for their grand future. For three years He was with them night and day, His energy devoted to the task of molding their characters. By personal influence He brought out what was finest in them and stamped His own likeness on them. What He did for the disciples He has been doing for successive generations of believing men and women right down the centuries. "But to all who received Him, who believed in His name, He gave power to become children of God."

XIII

The Importance of Being Third-Rate

When we read Jesus' parable of the talents, it is about the man endowed with five talents that most of us like to think. He was able, enterprising, successful, which is what we would all wish to be. In the story, however, the person on whom interest is concentrated is neither the man of outstanding ability, nor the man of marked ability, but the man of average ability.

Henry A. Wallace called this the century of the Common Man. But, in America, who wants to be common? It is taken for granted that every normal young person will strive to get on, climb the social ladder, outstrip his competitors in the walk of life he has chosen. The Horatio Alger tradition dies hard—from obscurity to distinction, from rags to riches, from Log Cabin to White House.

Ambition is, of course, an admirable quality, but only so long as it is rightly motivated and directed toward worthy ends. Too much can be made of it, as Cardinal Wolsey came to realize: "I charge thee, fling away ambition; by that sin fell the angels." Our Lord's parable is a reminder that there are sharp limits to human capacity. The majority of men and women are endowed neither with five talents nor with two but with one. Forgetting this, parents frequently make unreasonable demands on their children. They expect a brilliance they never achieved themselves and of which in their children there is little sign in native endowment or actual performance. There are children who endeavor with pathetic persistence to measure up to their parents' ambitions for them and reproach themselves when, through no fault of their own and not for want of trying, they fall short.

"All men," says the Declaration of Independence, "are created equal." True, but in what sense? Rudyard Kipling wrote

> For the Colonel's Lady an' Judy O'Grady
> Are sisters under their skins!

We are all equal in that we have a common origin. We are all without distinction of class, color or race, children of God. We are all equal in worth to God. That is the Christian source and inspiration of democracy—though a simple equation of the two is not justified. On that ground—the Fatherhood of God, the Brotherhood of Man—we all have equal and inalienable rights to life, liberty, and the pursuit of happiness, and should have equal opportunities. But we are *not* all equal in native capacity and ability. Brain power varies from person to person as does poetic genius, and artistic skill, and business acumen, and force of personality. There are far more third-rate authors, scientists, statesmen, lawyers, doctors, engineers, and salesmen than first-rate ones. The fact, though obvious, is repeatedly ignored.

It is foolish to ignore it and can result in chronic unhappiness. Every individual ought to attempt a balanced appraisal of himself. He should be at pains to be objective in self-judgment and should take a realistic attitude toward his capacities and gifts. For most of us this means ridding ourselves of delusions of grandeur, acknowledging and accepting the fact that we don't have first-class minds, that we can't now and never will turn in the top-flight performance of which genius is capable. C. P. Snow, the novelist, writes about one of his characters, a nuclear physicist, "His research was sound but, judged by high standards, while what he was doing was good it was not quite *good enough.*" The physicist's elder brother was deeply disappointed, for he had invested so much hope in him, including hopes of his own that had been frustrated. The physicist himself had humbler expectations. He was ready to come to terms with his talents, to be sorry they were not greater, but to make the best of them.

Surely that is the sensible, practical course to follow. Most of us are modestly endowed, and we shall not achieve effectiveness or happiness until we recognize it and are content with less than the rosy dreams of our youth had promised. Some refuse to recognize the facts about themselves, are reluctant to come to terms with their limited talents, and make a pathetic attempt at inflating their ego, mostly by bluffing and boasting. A man served in the army during the last war and achieved the rank of Private First Class. When he was demobilized he bored his long-suffering wife and family with tales of his heroic exploits when in combat. It was his youngest daughter who finally deflated him. "Daddy," she asked, "did you have anyone helping you to beat the Germans?"

There are those who, when the hour of rude awakening comes and they are forced to face the facts about themselves, instead of taking their measure, objectively appraising their accomplishments and then making the most of what they have and are, develop feelings of inferiority. They become the prey of discouragement and despondency. A sense of insignificance overwhelms them. They say to themselves, Here am I— a nonentity, counting for nothing, influencing nobody. What is the use of competing with people who can leave me far behind without even exerting themselves?

Finding themselves in a bog of discouragement and despondency, they may give way to envy and jealousy and self-exoneration. Unhappy over being left behind in the race, they are sour toward those who have forged ahead of them. "He has the advantage of money—he ought to get on." "He has had influence back of him at every turn, friends at court who pushed and procured preferment for him. I have always been on my own." "He has had all the 'breaks'—no wonder he has made a name for himself." So self-pity goes hand in hand with depression. Alibis and rationalizations are invented to prevent loss of "face." One has to deal, in short, with an embittered and unhappy individual.

Because he is embittered and unhappy the chances are that he will stop trying. The man with one talent, looking resentfully at those who have five or two, is prone to say, "With my limited capacity, little can be expected of me." What is worse, he expects little of himself. Since he is not able to achieve anything very great, he does not bestir himself to achieve anything at all. Because he cannot shine, he begins to whine and to recline. He grows lazy, indolent, disinclined to make any special effort. Ask him to undertake a responsible task, a task to which he can do justice if he applies himself, and he tells you that he doesn't feel he is the person for the job and that there are others more competent. His instinctive recoil from responsibility is due not to modesty but to lack of drive, initiative, and resourcefulness. He has stopped trying. Natural capacities have been extirpated by disuse. He had one talent, but even that has been taken from him.

In all this, what needs to be emphasized is that the work of the world is done by men and women of modest ability. It is on their shoulders that the brunt of the burden and toil of carrying on the whole complicated business of life falls. Lincoln said that God must love common people because He made so many of them. We need the genius, but we need the ordinary man as well. The architect cannot make the cathedral come to life without the bricklayer. Shakespeare cannot become current coin without the printer and bookbinder. The captain of industry cannot begin to function without scores of employees going about their humdrum tasks with diligence and conscientiousness. At one time a good deal was heard about Princes of the Pulpit. What would the Church of Christ in America do without its small-town preachers?

About one such preacher, his famous son, Roland Bainton, has written:

His congregations never numbered more than 200. He was an inconspicuous minister. He was a contented minister. Early he realized that he would never play a conspicuous role in the life of the Church. Had he been invited to a renowned pulpit he could not have accepted by reason of the infirmities of the flesh. He suffered from glandular tuberculosis in college, and though this was surmounted he continued to be sickly. . . . One thus hampered could not have carried a major assignment. [He] knew it and was not cankered by jealousy, tormented by ambition or racked by frustration. Within the framework of frailty he aimed at excellence, reminding himself that . . . "the wayside pool reflects the fleeting clouds as exactly as does the mighty ocean."

Who was it said, "Make no more giants, Lord, but elevate the race"? "I think," wrote Charles Darwin, "that I could make something of a case against the enormous importance which we attribute to our greatest men. I have been accustomed to think second, third and fourth rate men of very high importance, at least in science." And by way of illustration there is the case of Marconi claiming that his epoch-making discoveries would have been impossible but for the work of a humble and unknown scientist named Tay. Think of what James Barrie owed to his mother. Think of what David Livingstone owed to the handful of Africans who were his faithful, devoted companions on expedition after expedition. What would Paul have accomplished without Silas, Timothy, Epaphroditus, Aristarchus? Great men stand on the shoulders of little men. Their superlative achievement is rooted in the faithfulness of the unknown and the obscure. Who can tell how much prominent personages in church and state owe to some village schoolmaster or country minister or Sunday School teacher?

So in His parable, Jesus concentrates attention neither on the man with five talents nor on the man with two but on the man with one. Again and again in the Gospels, He extols the worth of what the world calls "obscure" service. He especially commends those who are faithful in little things. He says that a cup of cold water given in love—it was a proverbial expression for a minor service—will not go unrewarded. He singles out for honorable mention those who feed the hungry, visit the sick, care for prisoners. His heart always went out to the common man performing a common task faithfully and well. He taught that God judges not by success but by endeavor, not by brilliance but by fidelity. His standards are not our standards. On the Day of Judgment, when the books are opened and men are called to account, many who were first will be last, and the last, first.

What is required of us is that we make the most of such gifts as we possess. One of the finest tributes ever paid to anybody was expressed in six words: "She has done what she could." That is more than a eulogy. Implicit in it is a challenge, a stringent demand. Our ability is the measure of our responsibility. By that standard, by what we have it in us to be and do, we shall be judged at the last. God is not a hard taskmaster. The Divine demand is not unreasonable. We shall not be blamed for having only one talent. We are not asked to do the impossible, but we are asked to do what we can. With God, capacity and obligation are commensurate.

There has never been a man utterly devoid of some talent. We are not all gifted alike but each of us has some distinctive endowment, aptitude, quality of mind or spirit. Rudyard Kipling made the point in quaint, humorous fashion:

> There's not a pair of legs so thin, there's not a head so thick,
> There's not a hand so weak and white, nor yet a heart so sick,
> But it can find some needful job that's crying to be done
> For the glory of the Garden glorifieth every one.

We all have some talent, and the business of life is to discover what it is. Then, having discovered what it is, we are to put it to maximum use. In the words of Paul to young Timothy, we are to stir up the gift of God that is in us. When all is said and done this is the acid test of any character. Is it not also the criterion of true Christian discipleship? Recognizing this, Edward Hale declared:

> I am only one,
> But still I am one.
> I cannot do everything,
> But still I can do something;
> And because I cannot do everything
> I will not refuse to do the something
>   that I can do.

It is required of a steward, the Bible says, that he be found faithful—not brilliant, illustrious, successful, but faithful.

XIV

How to Handle Our Handicaps

Lord Byron and Sir Walter Scott were both lame. Byron was embittered by his lameness, brooded on it till he loathed it, never entered a public place but his mind reverted to it, so that much of the color and zest of existence were lost to him. Scott, on the other hand, never complained or spoke one bitter word about his disability, not even to his dearest friend. In the circumstances it is not so very surprising that Sir Walter should have received a letter from Byron with this sentence in it: "Ah Scott, I would give all my fame to have your happiness."

We all have handicaps of some sort. They may be physical, mental, temperamental. The important thing is to learn how to handle them. Above everything else *try not to give way to bitterness*. The odds against you are doubled if you allow a handicap—poor health, limited opportunity, a personality problem—to make you resentful, your face sullen, your chin down, your shoulders sagging. Yet this is what some do. They go about with a sense of grievance, complain that life has dealt them a raw deal, has never given them what others have received or what they consider their due. Bitterness works like poison. It is as liable to cause disease as any germ. It breeds touchiness, hypersensitivity, hostility.

On Broadway one night when the traffic light turned green, I made to help a blind man across the road. He turned on me instantly and in invective-laden language told me to mind my own business. He was having a sore time handling an uncommonly heavy handicap, but bitterness was only doubling the odds against him. If I could have got his ear I wonder whether it would have been helpful to tell him about Dr.

Barnardo. His son died of diphtheria when nine years of age. At first Barnardo may have been resentful and rebellious but he mastered the mood and rose above it. Grieving over the loss of his little boy he made a vow that he would, by God's grace, consecrate himself to the service of small children. The Barnardo Orphan Homes were the result.

For another type of handicap the important thing to say is, *Don't let the sense of inferiority take hold of you.* There are people of all ages who have allowed their handicaps—poor appearance, low-grade intellectual ability, ill-health—to limit drastically their horizons. They have far too quicky come to terms with themselves and their limitations. The psychologists very properly insist on the need of self-acceptance, but there is a self-acceptance that is altogether too supine and indolent. Few things are sadder than to see men and women losing heart and hope, drifting into apathy and inertia, deliberately sentencing themselves to low levels of achievement. I am not minimizing their handicap. I am saying that when it begets a sense of inferiority, frustration and inaction are too frequently the result. Whatever the handicap, the fact remains that the person who imposes a strict discipline on himself becomes a better person and does finer work. He may have decided limitations, but he neither feels superfluous nor useless. He keeps his self-respect. As was pointed out in the preceding chapter, there is no dishonor in having only one talent whereas others have five or ten. The dishonor lies in neglecting and failing to turn to full account whatever the gift that has been entrusted to one's care.

But all such counsel—try not to give way to bitterness, don't let the sense of inferiority get you down—is negative. Look at the other aspect of the case, the positive aspect. *Think of the men and women who have triumphed over their handicaps.* Paul, for example. Ailing, frail, weakened by hunger and often by fever, he completed a lifework that, as a mere physical performance, compels admiration. About it Adolf Deissmann wrote:

I had the great happiness and privilege of going over almost all the routes traversed by St. Paul; one of the most lasting impressions derived from these journeys, which were mostly made with modern means of locomotion, is my unspeakable amazement at the purely physical accomplishment of St. Paul the traveller, who truly might say not without reason that he buffeted his body and brought it into subjection like a slave.

All of us have heard of William James and Henry James, two brilliant brothers, but what do we know of their sister Alice? She was a real person in her own right. An invalid from her eighteenth year to the year of her early death at forty, she knew all about handicaps. But you could never tell if you went through her journal that she was a bedridden invalid. Reading George Eliot's letters, which contain frequent references to aches and pains, she asked, "Where was the creature's pride?" About Alice James, her biographer comments, "She never accepted the horizons of invalidism." The mind has unbelievable powers over the body.

I could so easily go on multiplying instances. A library of books could be assembled about men and women who have triumphed over their handicaps. They have had a hard time and few advantages but have won their way through to distinction. They have gone through life incapacitated in one way or another, but they have nevertheless produced some of the finest work in every sphere of activity. Milton was blind. Beethoven was deaf. Darwin was (the words are his own) "almost continually unwell." These are great names, but the triumph is not confined to the great ones of the earth. I knew a student, a girl, a victim of infantile paralysis, whose body was cruelly distorted and whose every movement was labored, but whose personality was radiant and whose academic record gave no hint of the difficulties she had to contend with. And there is the story of the man, obscure and unknown but typical of countless persons, who was blinded in a motor accident. His first thoughts afterward were angry, resentful, rebellious thoughts. But by the time of the major operation, when the doctor told him that he could save only part of one eye, and that the other eye would have to be taken out and a glass eye put in, he surprised even himself by replying, "All right, Doctor, I consent, but if you do have to put in a glass eye please put a twinkle in it."

We often say that such gallant souls have triumphed *over* their handicaps. Ought we not rather to say that they have triumphed *because* of them? The handicap has in so many instances proved more of an incentive than an impediment. All over this country are men ready to testify that the success they have achieved in their profession or business they owe to the challenge of early disadvantages. The very obstacles in their path were what put them on their mettle and stirred in them resolution and grit.

> Doubtless [James Barrie told the students of St. Andrew's University] the Almighty could have provided us with better fun than hard work, but I don't know what it is. To be born poor is probably the next best thing. The greatest glory that has ever come to me was to be swallowed up in London, not knowing a soul, with no means of subsistence, and the fun of working till the stars went out.

In such a school for character, a man visibly takes on stature; his mind develops, his powers mature. One of the Scottish clans has for its motto *Sub pondere cresco,* "I grow under the burden." Instead of giving way to bitterness or slumping into inertia the thing to do with a handicap is *to accept and use it.* There is no limitation, no misfortune, no burden of sorrow or sickness or suffering that the human spirit cannot rise above. These things, after all, are the raw material out of which character is made. Resentment, cynicism, self-pity need not be the reaction. Booker T. Washington again and again made use of the phrase, "the advantages of disadvantages," a phrase illumined for us when we think of Helen Keller, blind and deaf, saying, "I thank God for my handicaps, for through them I have found myself, my work and my God."

Nobody can miss the point of all this. It can be summarized in a sentence. *Granted the handicap, do the very best you can with what you have.* The man who had only one talent was at a disadvantage compared with the person who had five and the other person who had ten. But he *had* one talent, and it was given for use. We are not all gifted alike, but everybody has a gift of some kind.

Harold Russell had his hands blown off by the blast of a TNT blockbuster. Lying in a hospital, it terrified him to think of going through life with steel hooks instead of hands. There were days when he didn't care much whether he lived or died. Then he had a visitor, Charley McGonegal, who had lost his own hands in World War I. (Doesn't it move you to think of that meeting? It takes adversity to understand adversity.) One thing McGonegal told Russell which lingered in his memory, "You are not crippled; you are merely handicapped." At the first opportunity Russell was looking up the two words in a dictionary. Crippled meant "disabled, incapable of proper or effective action." Handicapped meant "any disadvantage or hindrance making success in an undertaking more difficult."

Russell seized on the distinction. Everything was not over. He could still achieve success. There and then he began a new chapter of his life, resolved to do the best with what he had. Here in his own words is his commentary on this sentence from Emerson: "For everything you have missed, you have gained something too." He says:

My weakness—my handlessness—my sense of inferiority—has turned out to be my greatest strength. I didn't think so at the time it happened and I don't think I'd ever willingly lose my hands, if I had to do it all over again. But having lost them I feel perhaps I have gained many fine things I might never have had with them. . . . This seeming disaster has brought me a priceless wealth of the spirit that I am sure I could never have possessed otherwise. I have enjoyed a life that has been full and rich and rewarding, a life that has had a meaning and depth it never had before. . . . *It is not what you have lost, but what you have left that counts.*

Using to the full what was left, doing the best with what he had, Russell, acting, writing, lecturing, speaking on the radio, has developed talents and abilities he never dreamed he possessed, and might never have discovered but for the loss of his hands.

I am concerned with a topic like this to do more than teach Stoic doctrine. To the heavily handicapped, the advice of the Stoic is: Keep your chin up and your shoulders squared and don't give in. You find it in Marcus Aurelius and Epictetus and Seneca—strong, robust doctrine with the emphasis all on self-reliance. But when Paul labored under his handicap, had to live with his thorn in the flesh, he found he needed to get down to a deeper level. He was a strong personality, but self-reliance was not enough. He besought the Lord thrice that the thorn might be removed. It was no removed. Whatever it was, he had to carry it with him to his dying day. But his prayer did not go unanswered. This was the answer: "My grace is sufficient for you, for my power is made perfect in weakness."

If your problem is the handling of a heavy handicap, be sure to get beyond self-reliance to that deeper level where your life is open to the grace of God. An atheist is a man without invisible means of support. A Christian draws on resources that are Divine. "Jesus Christ came into my room last night," wrote Samuel Rutherford from a dark dungeon in the city of Aberdeen, "and every stone shone like a ruby." Abraham Lincoln, leaving Springfield for the White House, the burden of office heavy on him, reached that deeper level, for, addressing friends and associates, he told them, "Without Divine assistance I cannot succeed; with it I cannot fail." When you have accepted your handicaps and sought to use them, when you have done the best you can with what you have, be sure, be very sure, to turn to the greatest resource of all: "My grace is sufficient for you, for my power is made perfect in weakness."

Part Three
TOWARD A RELEVANT FAITH

XV

Are Americans Growing Soft?

Paul in the first century counseled Timothy to "endure hardness, as a good soldier of Jesus Christ." It is sound counsel in any century. Americans today should especially take it to heart. Edmund Burke said that an indictment was not to be drawn up against a whole people. Generalizations should always and rightly be suspect, for they take no account of exceptions, and the exceptions are too numerous and too weighty to be disregarded. Even so, it is arguable that the *trends* in America just now are in the direction of slackness and laxness. Sweeping assertions are unjustified, but pertinent questions are in order.

Are Americans growing soft *physically?* Are Americans becoming enamored of comfort, ease, and affluence? Are Americans spending too much on luxuries and too little on essentials —schools, hospitals, public housing, research, economic aid to Asia and Africa, the arts, deserving causes? Do Americans want to buy everything ready-made—food, clothes, education, music, pleasure? Has a cult of soft living been substituted for the pioneer psychology?

Not long ago one of the men who interviews college seniors for employment after graduation was asked how he went about the task. He said that he made a practice of inquiring, "What are your goals, what do you want out of life?" He cited the case of a student whose answer was: "Well, I'd like a nice wife, a couple of kids, a home in Westchester, or somewhere around New York. They have good schools. Then I'd like to join the country club and be able to play golf or tennis on weekends. I don't know about becoming a millionaire, but I want to be comfortable." There is no mention in that prospectus of politics, religion, or community responsibility.

It may be objected that all college seniors are not like that one. That is true, but pick up a book like *The Ugly American*. Complaining of dilettanti and slackers in the American foreign service, it tells of a State Department pamphlet showing young people boarding sleek airplanes, bound for good, easy living, and shopping in exotic bazaars. "The pamphlet does not have a *single* word which indicates that the work will be demanding, not a *single* word to suggest that we are locked in a quiet struggle around the world, and that recruits will be part of that struggle. It is a pamphlet," the authors say, "designed to attract mediocrities." In contrast, *The Ugly American* is from first to last, a plea for hardworking and dedicated men and women—of whom it supplies splendid illustrations— willing to risk their creature comforts and their health in the service of their country and for the common good.

Hard work and dedication—that is where the emphasis should be put. Those were the qualities that laid the foundations of America. If I had my way I would make Irving Stone's epic story *Men to Match My Mountains* required reading for parents as well as their children. It is worth any number of the Westerns to be seen nightly on the television screen. The pioneers, subduing wild land, breaking up virgin prairies, were a hardy breed, their resourcefulness matched by their courage. The forward look is characteristic of Americans, yet a backward look now and then would help greatly in shaping goals. De Tocqueville came upon one of the pioneers on the farther reaches of the frontier, in the midst of a dark and untamed forest, sitting in his hut within reach of his ax and his rifle, alone by a candle, reading a book. The temptation today being in the direction of slackness and softness, the call is for more strenuous and disciplined living on the part of us all.

I ask another pertinent question. Are Americans growing soft *morally?* Here again generalizations have to be avoided. There is a tendency to paint the past in lily-white colors and the present in dark and somber hues. The fact is that in the days of the pioneers, professional requirements were low: the quack flourished in medicine, the shyster in law, the ignoramus in the ministry. Business frequently followed the maxim, *Caveat emptor,* "Let the buyer beware." David Harum quipped, "Do unto others as they would do unto you, and do it fust." Today in business and the professions the standards of legality are higher and men are more conscious that legality is not enough, that principle and honor are basic for a nation's well-being and security. Still, when this has been recognized, there is no gainsaying that the contemporary situation is disquieting.

Television scandals, fraudulent business practices, huckstering of high-pressure advertisers, corruption in political life at both the local and the national level—one could go on detailing instance after instance of graft, vice, the lust for quick money and big money, the lack of integrity. There are thousands upon thousands of law-abiding, honor-loving people in America, but these happenings are danger signals. They are symptoms, indicative of trends. They point in the direction of a depreciation of the moral currency. They are the symbols of a society in which the easy way, the get-something-for-nothing attitude, the shady deal, have become widely acceptable as long as it is possible to get away with them. They are a cancer eating at the vitals of American life which, if it goes on spreading, will bring this mighty nation low. What should cause the deepest concern at the moment is not technological backwardness but moral obtuseness. Without a culture which has values superior to money, without a robust moral sense, no nation can be strong.

I ask a third pertinent question. Are Americans growing soft *spiritually?* I am not thinking of the budgets raised by churches, or of the percentage of the population to be found in the churches on Sundays, or of the place maintained by volumes on religion at the top of the best-seller book lists. Paradoxically enough, considering what I have just been pointing out about moral obtuseness, religion is in a more flourishing condition in America than anywhere else in the

Western hemisphere. I am thinking of the ends for which churches are the means. I am thinking of national purpose, what it is that we want from life. Here the trends are most pronounced.

American goals are predominantly material. Grayson Kirk, president of Columbia University, says, "Somewhere along the line we have become fat, smug and spiritually anemic." What is meant by "spiritually anemic"? Too much taken up with the here and now, with things, with gadgets, with what can be seen, tasted, handled. We work harder for money than for anything else, and the way in which we spend it tells its own story; for example, 15 billion dollars for smoking and drinking in a year but only half a billion dollars more than that for education, only 3.7 billion dollars for religious and welfare activities combined.

Americans are a religious people, but church life is mostly a gratification, seldom a sacrifice. "Religion," somebody has said, "is an umbrella to protect us from the rain." That is the prevailing trend. People turn to religion as a remedy for sleeplessness, worry, and ineffectiveness, to be free from frustrations and tension, to become resourceful and successful. The presumption is that God exists to serve us, whereas our chief end in life is to serve God. And once we think of God as existing to serve us, our religion is comforting and comfortable. Passivity is then the word that best describes us. Our flabbiness is apparent in our apathy, complacency and inertia. It takes a great deal to rouse us, and we are not roused for long. Who would ever charge us with "turning the world upside down?" We are not noted for a crusading spirit or for reforming zeal. Bad men do not need to fear us, and evil can go on unchecked. We shoulder no cross, carry no banners, shun commitments and causes, conform to the world and its ways. To be sure, there are exceptions—prophets, saints, crusading citizens—but what are they among so many? A far cry all this from: "Endure hardness as a good soldier of Jesus Christ"; "Enter in at the strait gate"; "You have not yet resisted unto blood, striving against sin"; "If any man would come after me, let him deny himself and take up his cross daily and follow me."

Are Americans growing soft? The trend points in that direction. What a time for such a trend to show itself! We are locked in a desperate struggle around the world. A battle is going on for the minds and souls of men. Over against us, challenging us, competing with us, are the Communist powers, Russia disputing our leadership, China emulating Russia's example. A Canadian reporter's account of a visit to Communist China tells a sobering and in many ways frightening story, the story of 650 million people in process of regimentation, regimented to swat flies and kill mosquitoes because they spread disease, to build homemade blast furnaces in backyards and farm fields to produce iron and steel, 400,000 volunteers in the phenomenally short space of 160 days constructing the huge Ming Tu reservoir and dam. We are faced now by two great powers whose citizens are being bred to "scorn delights and live laborious days." Back in the thirties Dean Inge wrote, "The future belongs to nations with a lower standard of living and a higher standard of work than ours. We cannot hope to be always in a privileged position." No more, in the fateful sixties, can the United States. This is no time for slackness and laxness.

Since the trend points in that direction, where does responsibility for it lie? Responsibility for it is widespread. The *government* is involved. It has permitted private standards of life to be paramount over public standards. It will have to establish austerity standards, raising taxes not reducing them, so that less is spent on the "good things" of private life and more on the priorities. Our *schools and colleges* are involved, for, to quote Grayson Kirk again, too many of them have "virtually abdicated their functions in society because they are content to give their students little more than an opportunity to have pleasurable social experiences." Our *churches* are involved for there is a glaring discrepancy between their numerical and financial strength and their influence on American manners and morals. Our *public media* are involved—the infantilism of radio and television, the networks giving the public what they think the public wants, a dreary diet of violence, brutality, and sex, week in and week out.

Can nothing be done about the "yellow press"? Read by millions, plastering sordid tales of lust and crime over its front pages, retailing gossip and scandal in its middle pages, devoting inordinate coverage to sport, it debauches public taste and contributes directly to the softening of the moral fiber of the nation. Its proprietors are shockingly irresponsible and should hang their heads in shame over the lurid content of their newspapers. Have they no conscience? Are circulation and profit the only criteria? Christian people, practicing a justifiable discrimination, should boycott such rags.

When Carl Sandburg was presented with a gold medal for history and biography by the Academy of Arts and Letters he said, "We find it momentous that Lincoln used the word 'responsibility' nearly as often as he used the word 'freedom.'" Yes, momentous. We talk about free churches. We talk about a free press. We talk, as Frank Stanton of C.B.S. did lately, about public media free from any controls. We talk about free enterprise. Free for what? We need to ask: Who paid for our freedom? What was the price? We need a sense of responsibility to match and justify our freedom.

How does one deal with softness, physical, moral, spiritual? The answer is largely in one word, discipline. Marcus Aurelius was the best of what are known as the five good Roman emperors and his rule of life was, "Prefer the hard." That was George Washington's maxim also. We smile when we think of what Leslie Stephen remarked about his father: "He once smoked a cigar and found it so delicious that he never smoked again." It is absurd, we say, to be so suspicious of pleasure. But we tend to the other extreme; we are slack and self-indulgent, with our wishbone where our backbone should be. During the war when submarines were sinking American ships off the coast of Florida, and it was difficult to get hotel-keepers and casino operators to consent not to a black-out but to a brown-out, a newspaper correspondent wrote:

Some men die by shrapnel,
And some go down in flames,
But most men perish inch by inch,
Who play at little games.

If a country is to be as great morally and spiritually as it is materially, its citizenry must "scorn delights and live laborious days." It must produce men of the order of Dr. Thomas A. Dooley, founder of hospitals in Laos, who literally gave his life to the cause of healing the sick.

Arnold Toynbee is at work on the eleventh volume of his *Study of History.* He says that a large portion of the volume will be given to answering his critics and occasionally modifying the *Study* where he thinks the criticisms merit it. But he insists that the central thesis of the work will go untouched, that it is difficulties and obstacles which lead to the flowering of a civilization. Difficulties and obstacles at any stage of a civilization are met and mastered only where there is discipline.

Self-reverence, self-knowledge, self-control,
These three alone lead life to sovereign power.

This is especially true of those of us who are Christians. Our central symbol is a Cross. Our commitment is as rigorous as that of a marine on combat service. Think again of Paul's counsel to Timothy: "Endure hardness as a good soldier of Jesus Christ." Think, above all, of Christ's ultimatum, "If any man would come after me, let him deny himself and take up his cross daily and follow me."

XVI

On Hating Things, Not People

F. L. Lucas, in his fine book, *The Search for Good Sense*, maintains that we lavish on persons the hate that should be reserved only for things. He holds that it should be a matter of principle with us to hate things, not people. For hate, like atomic power, can be devastating when it is hate of people, but a vital source of energy when it is hate of things.

But should we hate at all? Doesn't hate of any kind work like a poison and leave the hater, the anti-Semite for instance, sick and neurotic? The Bible is emphatic in its answer. It says that there is "a time to love, and a time to hate." The quotation is from Ecclesiastes, which in many of its sentiments is sub-Christian, but the quotation does not stand alone. One of the psalmists makes bold to affirm that "the Lord loves those who hate evil." The prophet Amos bids his hearers "hate evil, and love good." He goes further and represents the Almighty as declaring, "I hate, I despise your feasts"—strong language to apply to temple worship services. It may be objected that these are quotations from the Old Testament, but the New Testament is no exception to the rule. In the Epistle to the Hebrews, Christ is described as loving righteousness and hating lawlessness. The church in Ephesus is commended for hating the works of the Nicolaitans—not the Nicolaitans themselves but their works. Not once or twice but many times God Himself is spoken of as a God of wrath and anger.

There is a hatred from which we instinctively recoil. In so many of its manifestations it is ugly, vicious, and destructive, doing fully as much harm to the subject as to the object, making ugly the soul of man, ravishing the face of the hater, twisting and warping his personality.

114

A story is told about the head of a college who resigned in a huff after three years' presidency, and later left all his property to another college. He may have been wronged, but the fact remains that although he had read great numbers of books in several languages, although he had lectured to hundreds of teachers' institutes on how to educate the young, although he had traveled three times around the world, somehow all his travel and lecturing and reading could not help him when his heart nursed a hate. Would it have made any difference if he had come across Emily Dickinson's lines?

> I had no time to hate, because
> The grave would hinder me,
> And life was not so ample I
> Could finish enmity.

It is pitiful to think of people going down to the grave nursing animosities that blight body, mind, and spirit.

On the other hand, there are *things* that should be hated, evil things that should rouse in us loathing and abhorrence. How can a Christian look on war, racism, slums, prostitution, economic exploitation with anything other than detestation? There is a hatred that is clean, disinterested, free from malice —a "perfect hatred" the Bible calls it. "My God," said General Bramwell Booth as he worked in the slums in the East End of London, "how I detest the enemy which has wrought this havoc." Without such indignation, selfless and righteous, rising to the boiling point, evil will go on flourishing. The passion I am describing is indispensable to moral leadership. The Reformers, when you think of them, were they not almost without exception angry men, God's angry men: Amos thundering against the oppression of the poor, Savonarola scourging Florence for its vice, Martin Luther at white heat assailing the evils of the Indulgence system, John Brown lashing in wrath at the iniquity of slavery? Disinterested hatred has had a part in all beneficial reforms and revolutions. It is not incongruous with love. Indeed, can we describe as either loving or good anyone who is incapable of hatred of wrongdoing? For a Christian, hatred of evil is not only permissible but mandatory.

There is a problem here: to hate and at the same time to love; to be angry and at the same time to be just; to rise up in righteous indignation against some flagrant iniquity and at the same time to preserve the Christian spirit; to follow the example of the Old Testament prophets who were fearless, uncompromising spokesmen for God and righteousness and at the same time to have the mind and disposition of Christ and His apostles for whom love was the fulfilling of the whole law. F. L. Lucas, to whose book I referred at the outset, offers a clue to the problem. We should hate things, not persons.

There was a memorable day in the old City Temple in London. It was at the time of the Armenian and Bulgarian atrocities. Feeling in Britain was mounting as, in the House of Commons, Gladstone brought the atrocities to light. Joseph Parker went into the pulpit of the City Temple and, denouncing them, cried, "God damn the Sultan!" In our own time, despite Christ's command, "Love your enemies," many were ready to vent the same malediction on Hitler, Mussolini, Stalin; many are ready now to wreak it on the leaders of Red China. Some time ago a European clergyman lamented that "men of high responsibility in the West," some of whom "say that they are Christians," do not hesitate to shake the hands of the oppressors of Hungary and other countries under Communist rule; they even introduce Communist leaders to the free world, not realizing that by so doing they "shake the hand that slapped the face of Christ." This is a reflection of the Old Testament at its lowest, not of the New Testament at its highest. This is not love of enemies; this would make pariahs of them.

> He drew a circle that shut me out—
> Heretic, rebel, a thing to flout.
> But Love and I had the wit to win:
> We drew a circle that took him in.

Of all war novels, *All Quiet on the Western Front* was one

of the most moving. There is a passage in it telling how once when a soldier was left behind in a shell hole, a heavy body stumbled and fell beside him. The soldier struck out with his bayonet; then he looked at his victim and said:

Comrade, I did not want to kill you, but you were only an idea to me before, an abstraction that lived in my mind. It was the abstraction that I stabbed, but now for the first time I see that you are a man like me, now I see your wife and your face and our fellowship. Forgive me, comrade; we always see it too late. Why do they never tell us that you are just poor devils like us, that your mothers are just as anxious as ours, that you have the same fear of death and the same dying and the same agony? If we threw away these rifles and the uniforms I could be your brother. If I come out of this I shall fight against this that has struck us both down.

That is where the emphasis should be. Evil things like war we should fight to the death, not the persons who so often are the helpless victims of war. At International Christian University in Tokyo they tell of a contribution received from an American whose son was killed at the hands of the Japanese in World War II. At first, the soul of the father was full of bitterness, but in time, and with relief, he saw that Japanese boys, like his own boy, had been helplessly caught up in the vortex that modern warfare is. His contribution to International Christian University was his attempt to cut at the root of the evil.

So often when hatred is vented on wrongdoers, the system that bred the wrong goes unchecked, is not dealt with drastically and surgically. We hunt for scapegoats and pillory them when we should be digging deeper and getting at the roots of our malaise and maladies. Senator Joseph McCarthy chased after scapegoats, and since his death has become one. There was a period when some of us were in trouble every time we ventured publicly to criticize him; now guilt is heaped on him that should lie heavy on us all. We take out our anger on individuals, blame them for our predicament, persuade ourselves that their exposure and punishment will make all well with us again, when we should be dealing with the diseases in our national life that are primarily responsible: the lust for easy money and big money, and the luxuries big money can buy; the lack of moral standards, of honesty, of truthfulness, of rectitude—wrong being wrong only when it is found out; the deplorably low taste of the general public reflected in the popularity of films and television programs featuring sex and violence. If only the indignation vented on scapegoats could be concentrated on the evils that breed them—what a transformation would be brought about in our common life!

The thing that is wanted badly in our time is a clean, disinterested hatred of evil. When one thinks of the wrongs that cry to high heaven to be set right, the apathy of the average citizen is astonishing. Carlyle used to complain of the "great big stupid public" on both sides of the Atlantic. Wrongs were done right under their eyes, and they kept silence, and by their silence acquiesced in the wrongs, permitted them to fester and multiply. It is perhaps in this respect that our age is most sadly deficient. We are too conformist, too submissive, too timidly silent. The fundamental decencies can be flouted or ignored, and we make no protest. The militarists go on year after year committing us ever more deeply to what is called ABC warfare, that is, war waged at the atomic, bacterial, and chemical levels, and our voice is not raised. When Martin Luther King was first putting up a gallant fight for his people in the South, it shocked him that more support did not come from Christians, particularly from Christian ministers. "History," he writes, "will have to record that the greatest tragedy of this period of social transition was not the strident clamor of the bad people, but the appalling silence of the good people. Our generation will have to repent not only for the acts and words of the children of darkness but also for the fears and apathy of the children of light."

What is the reason for this timid, culpable, criminal silence, the lack of righteous indignation, the absence of vigorous, passionate, horrified protest, of sharp, intelligent, constructive criticism? Why are we so prone to sit back and do nothing, to tolerate existing wrongs, to be neutral, to compro-

mise, to take the line of least resistance? How has it come
about that C. Wright Mills, professor of sociology at Columbia
University, can maintain: "Neither preachers nor the religious laity matter; what they do and what they say can be
readily agreed with and safely ignored"? A Sunday School
teacher suddenly stopped reading a passage in the Bible and
asked the youngsters: "Why do you believe in God?" She got
a variety of answers, some full of simple faith, others obviously
insincere. The one that stunned her came from the son of a
padre. He answered apologetically, "I guess it just runs in our
family." Is that the reason? Is the faith of the majority of
Protestants, Roman Catholics, and Jews an heirloom, a matter of tradition, a tradition accorded respect and taking for
granted belief in God and in moral and spiritual values, but
with no passion in it, no white hot fervor, neither ardent love
of right nor burning hatred of wrong?

On an Egyptian tomb, when the first dynasty was falling
into ruins, someone inscribed the words: "And no one is
angry enough to speak out." The same situation obtained
when Greece plummeted from its high estate into decline and
decay—liberty lost, democracy at an end, the Macedonians
achieving hegemony. Worse than the moral degeneracy of the
minority was the inertia of the majority. They could be
alarmed but not aroused. Only what touched their pockets
made them angry. Corruption and injustice in the body politic
went unmolested. Small men and women absorbed in small
pursuits could not keep the greatness of Greece alive. For that
there would have had to be the fire of conviction, and the fire
had gone out.

The lesson in all this should not be lost on us. The danger
besetting America, outlined in an earlier chapter, is that we
may become morally and spiritually flabby. Some think that
is what we have already become. One thing is clear. A moral
slump will not be averted unless there is an end of conformity,
submissiveness, and timid silence; unless there is a rebirth of
spiritual conviction; a revival among us of intense hatred of
evil in all its manifestations, of sharp, unsparing, intelligent

criticism of irresponsibility and immorality. In a time when basic human rights are openly denied—as in racism and anti-Semitism—and when basic moral principles are treated with contempt, we need prophetic voices to specify and confront real issues, to rouse moral and social concern, to challenge and bring to the surface all that is deepest and best in the American people.

Think of Christ. Speak of hating things not people, and He comes at once to mind. He recoiled from evil with abhorrence and scourged it with scathing speech. But for Him it was not enough to denounce evil. He knew how futile denunciation by itself can be. It may not help the evildoer to see and condemn himself. The way to open a man's eyes to badness is by the light of goodness. So Christ did not stop at denunciation of evil. He went further. He countered it, not by force and retaliation but by goodness and love; not by shedding blood but by letting His own blood be shed. And in so doing, by His death on the Cross, He exposed evil as no one else has ever done, and turned men from it to goodness as no one else has ever done. This was what so profoundly moved Gandhi, and was a factor in committing him, for life, to nonkilling and nonviolence. Sooner or later this is the high way which mankind must take—evil quickly and passionately resented, but instead of venting revenge and hatred on the evildoer, those wronged will rather suffer on his behalf.

Who is sufficient for these things? It is hard to be a Christian. "The Galilean is still too great for our hard hearts." But His way is the high way, the only way, to the better world.

XVII

Maintaining Independence
Despite Social Compulsion

American society has turned a slow-motion somersault. The rugged individualism which played such a decisive part in the making and building up of the nation is fast disappearing. The self-made man has been displaced by the organization man. The individual counts for less and less and the group for more and more. The emphasis is on belonging and adjustment—belonging to the group, adjusting to the organization. Executives in business, in government, in the universities, in research institutes, are well-rounded men, chosen by well-rounded men, who in turn seek out and select for promotion other well-rounded men. Wives of executives, according to an article in *Life* magazine, are no exception. They, too, must be screened to determine their suitability and adjustability. As a corporation official put it, "We've got quite an equity in the man, and it's only prudence to protect it by bringing the wife into the picture."

Did you read William H. Whyte's book *The Organization Man*, David Riesman's *The Lonely Crowd* or Vance Packard's *The Hidden Persuaders?* All three books illustrate the change that is taking place in the American character. Once people were innerdirected; now they are outerdirected and overdirected. It is becoming increasingly difficult to maintain independence and individuality because of social compulsion. The temptation, sensed instinctively by many a youth on the threshold of his career, is to settle into the customary grooves, to abide by established rules and patterns. The trend to conformity is pronounced—in literature, films, town planning, the suburbs, the activities of the churches.

When we think of the factors that have made this the generation of conformity, one stands out: the advertising agencies. In our day, they are the major wielders of social control. There are no tastemakers so powerful. More than any other influence at work in contemporary life they are pushing Americans toward the mediocrity that results from conformity. They are dictating the content of radio and television programs. By means of those media they are bombarding all of us, are bombarding children from the moment they can listen and just barely read. There is no doubt at all that these hidden and irresponsible persuaders are treating human beings as a commodity to be trafficked in—analyzed, manipulated, exploited, as in the case of the wretched giveaway programs. During the 1956 presidential campaign, Adlai Stevenson made the explosive comment: "The idea that you can merchandise candidates for high office like breakfast cereal . . . is the ultimate indignity to the democratic process."

This is one of the most pernicious and vulgarizing influences operating on American manners and morals. It is frightening in the extent to which it is making passive conformists of us. It is using psychiatry and the social sciences to get inside the subconscious for the "psychological hook" which will impel consumers by the million to buy what is advertised. Approximately sixty dollars a year is being spent on each man, woman, and child in America solely to coax him or her to use products the admen are promoting. From that angle the money is not being spent in vain. Why will American housewives pay $1.50 for a jar of skin cream, but only 25 cents for a bar of soap? An advertising executive explains. Soap promises only to make them clean whereas the cream promises to make them glamorous. Why are 65 per cent of all smokers absolutely loyal to one brand of cigarette and 20 per cent relatively loyal? In tests where cigarettes were masked, people could identify their brand by only 2 per cent better than chance. *They are smoking an image.* Puppetlike they are doing what they are told, and puppetlike they don't know they are being manipulated.

The story is told of a Syrian and an American who were sitting together in the salon of a Mediterranean liner when the ship's orchestra began to play the march tune, "The Parade of the Wooden Soldiers." The Syrian gravely and courteously rose and stood at attention. Puzzled, the American asked him what had got him to his feet. The Syrian answered, "I thought it was your national anthem." He was not joking. He had mistaken the tune. He honestly thought that "The Parade of the Wooden Soldiers" was the American national anthem. Is it, in point of fact, a sort of national anthem? To what degree are we free in the sense of being able to direct our own lives? Are social pressures flattening out independence and individuality, the qualities so characteristic of American character and life in the past? Is Sloan Wilson's *The Man in the Gray Flannel Suit* accurate as description and diagnosis? Is the typical student today a conformist, preoccupied with material values—security, a lucrative post, a comfortable family life? For a great number of Americans, is their church an appendix to their politics or to that vague generalization, the American way of life? What lies behind the dislike of differences, the intolerance of critical opinion, the disposition to define subversive activity in terms so broad that it includes all disliked ideas: the United Nations, foreign aid, pacifism, socialism, integration? I raise these questions because what is at stake is the dignity and freedom of the individual, the American ideal of free expression safeguarded in the Constitution, the right of every man under God to do his own thinking, listen to his own conscience, utter his own convictions, stand on his own feet.

A Sunday School teacher dared to take an opinion poll on the integration question when there were more than one hundred persons present. What was the result? Primarily, unanimous agreement that segregation is anti-Christian and anti-democratic; unanimous agreement that integration inevitably is coming; nearly unanimous opinion that they would oppose its coming in their lifetime; majority opinion that they hoped it would not come in the lifetime of their children; less than a dozen ready for integration now or at any time. Secondarily, an appeal to the teacher to get back to "teaching the Bible." That Sunday School teacher had individuality and independence, but they must be difficult to maintain in the face of an almost overwhelming social compulsion. This is the problem with which scores upon scores of ministers are living just now. It is the problem ministers are facing who believe that the present race in missile-making is civilization's crowning folly. For those in all walks of life who prefer praise to criticism, popularity to opposition, the *status quo* to any kind of controversy, for those who hesitate to take a course that will irritate or alienate others, conformity is the easier option. All of us are caught up in this trend to some extent. We don't want to be different, odd, eccentric. Asked when he was about eight what he was going to be, Thoreau replied, "I'll be I." He has a word for us today. "If a man does not keep pace with his companions, perhaps it is because he hears a different drummer. Let him step to the music which he hears, however measured or far away."

One thing is beyond dispute. Every great historic change has been based on nonconformity. Jesus was crucified because He was a nonconformist. If He had held His tongue, if He had been prepared to compromise, if He had let the powers that be alone and not castigated them as foxes, hypocrites, whited sepulchers, instead of dying at thirty-three He might have lived to be as white-haired as Caiaphas or as venerable as any of the religious leaders who handed Him over to Pilate. If tradition is to be believed, not many of the Apostles died in their beds; they, too, were nonconformists. "We must obey God rather than men," they said. They were caught in the first great loyalty test when they refused to sprinkle a little incense on the altar of Caesar. Without nonconformity there would have been no Reformation. Luther, Zwingli, Calvin, Knox, did not keep pace with their companions because they heard a different drummer and stepped to the march which they heard. Without nonconformity we should never have had a Bill of Rights, nor before that a

Magna Charta, nor before that a Bible. Society needs the critic, the visionary, the revolutionary.

While I was traveling in the Far East recently, this was something I thought about frequently, for I many times met leaders who had been imprisoned because of their convictions. Noting their fire and fervor, comparing it with the placidity and stolidity that in some cases characterize church leaders, I wondered whether persecution might not be the best thing that could happen to Christianity. A Dominican friar said to a group of young priests he was addressing, "If some of you are not careful you will die in your beds, and it will serve you right." A prominent clergyman in Britain, asked why he did not take the lead and speak out in wartime, acknowledged, "If I had said what was in my mind I should have been in prison in a week." In New York, W. E. Orchard told a group of seminarians, "Gentlemen, I am 65 years of age. I have never been in a prison; I have not been burnt alive, or shot at dawn; or stoned by the mob. You may guess that I have been playing my cards very carefully." And then he added, "Every good man today has to explain why he is alive." That may strike you as melodramatic, though surely not if you stop to think of the graveyards in Europe and Asia with their row upon row of white crosses. At any rate, you cannot deny that the people who have done most for the world and lifted the level of life in their generation have been the nonconformists.

This has been true of the Church in its greatest eras. Not all of its eras have been great. There have been long periods when it acquiesced in what was worldly and conventional, when it reflected the thought and practice of the period, when it was difficult to know what ideal of life it stood for other than a tolerant acceptance of the *status quo* with a mild desire that things should grow better in time so far as that was compatible with the maintenance of existing vested interests. A hundred years after this, historians may describe the Church of today in terms like those. With poverty, illiteracy, disease, bad government prevalent over more than half of the world, with civilization bent on the manufacture of armaments capable of obliterating itself, they may ask why the Church was so lackadaisical, so conformist, so much the submissive servant and mouthpiece of the spirit of the age. But at its best, the Church has spurned conformity with the world. It has not sought to adapt and accommodate itself to the times. It has not trimmed its message to current thought or to current social trends. It changed the whole outlook of the old Roman world. It transformed the barbarian tribes to whom its missionaries carried the Gospel. At the Reformation it struck a blow for soul-liberty and freedom of conscience. In revival after revival it created new ideals, new convictions, new characters, new power that made men different and made their generation different. The great epochs in the Church's history were not epochs when it made common cause with the world but when it stood over against the world, fearlessly proclaiming the Word of God manifested in Jesus Christ.

Today, as in any age, freedom from conformity should be the distinguishing mark of the Christian. "But ye are . . . a peculiar people," the Apostle Peter told the first Christians. There was no fear in New Testament days of eccentricity or of being different. The first Christians were unreconciled to life as they knew it. Their critics complained that they were disturbers of the peace, revolutionaries, who were turning the world upside down. So it has been right down the centuries. Think of Martin Luther before the Holy Roman Emperor, of John Bunyan before the courts of England, of Martin Niemöller before Hitler. Think of John Howard and his work in prisons, of David Livingstone, that most iconoclastic of missionaries, of Trevor Huddleston, Michael Scott, Martin Luther King. Such souls, pioneers all, are the true moral aristocrats, listening for and unhesitatingly obeying the voice of God. The world is full of conscript minds, but they have resisted the contagion. Unpurchasable men, they spearhead the thrust toward a new society.

What is their secret? What made nonconformists of them? What transformed and daily renewed their minds? This above all—their association with Jesus Christ, the great revolutionary. If you want, not to take character from your environment but to put character into it, you need to draw on spiritual resources greater than your own. And they are available. Paul, who said, "Do not be conformed to this world but be transformed by the renewal of your mind," and whose life is an inspiring illustration of that principle, discloses the secret in another of his sayings, "We have the mind of Christ."

Does someone say: "But how can I have the mind of Christ?" There are the Gospels. Do you read them? There is the Church which He founded. Do you belong to it, and faithfully serve it? There is the School of Prayer. Are you a pupil in it? Cried Coleridge, "Do not talk to me of the evidences for Christianity. Try it." That is the way to have the mind of Christ.

XVIII

The Use and Abuse of Leisure

Busy as we nearly all believe ourselves to be, we have more leisure at our disposal than any previous generation has known. The length of the working day is steadily being reduced. A forty-hour week is now common, and automation will probably reduce it within the lifetime of the rising generation to thirty or twenty-five hours. Teenagers have simply no notion of the conditions under which their forebears toiled. In his diary, John Clifford, born in Victorian England, stated: "I have worked from four o'clock on Friday morning all through the night to six o'clock on Saturday evening, and then run home glad and proud with my small wage of two shillings and sixpence to my mother—like a king." The work was to splice the ends of cotton from bobbin to bobbin to keep the thread unbroken.

Those days, thank God, have gone. With the advent of the Welfare State and the social legislation accompanying it, leisure in America has become an almost universal commodity. Most people have three times as much free time as working time. If this strikes you as fantastic, figure it out for yourself, subtracting the hours you work in any week from 168, the number of hours in a week. Much of the time, of course, is spent in sleeping and eating, but those are leisure activities. Three times as much free time as working time! Think about that, about the amount of leisure you have and what you are doing with it.

This is a vastly important subject. In Britain not long ago the House of Lords gave a whole day to a debate on the *problem* of leisure. First a personal problem, it has taken on the dimensions of a large-scale social problem. During the Industrial Revolution the picture was of employees like Clifford laboring from dawn until dusk six days a week, and wretchedly paid for their labor. Today the picture is that of the well-fed, well-clothed wage earner with a lot of spare time on his hands, and tending to fritter it away aimlessly, foolishly, selfishly. Often he has escaped from drudgery only to fall into the worse bondage of boredom. Overheard on the street was a remark addressed sharply by a wife to her husband: "What are you hurrying for? We're not going anywhere."

Triviality is perhaps the most characteristic and besetting sin of Americans: time frittered away in a succession of activities that lack any serious purpose; people at the end of the day complaining of exhaustion, having to be entertained but with no skill in entertaining themselves, possessing a pitifully small stock of interests, ideas, emotions. In this connection, television—which could be such an educative and cultural force—inclines instead to be a demoralizing influence. It has invaded our homes, and consumes more and more of our leisure hours. Said John Crosby, when he was with the *New York Herald Tribune,* "If the Harris committee wants to know what is wrong with television, it ought to stop interviewing witnesses and look at that monstrous box for a week." "Monstrous box" is no exaggeration. In support, Crosby quotes Clare Boothe Luce regarding the television fare of only a few years ago:

Today there are 27 Western and 20 Whodunits on the weekly programs of the major networks. For a thousand and more nights, from sea to shining sea, their chilling hordes have passed before the eyes of 42½ million American families. Among their evil numbers are safeblowers, brain blowers, convicts, extortioners, counterfeiters, blackmailers, thugs, gangsters, stool pigeons, hoodlums, savages, cattle rustlers, trigger-happy cowpokes, lynchers, jailbreakers, adventurers, drunks, drug addicts, pushers, pads, panderers, pimps, housebreakers, homebreakers, arsonists, sadists, psychopaths, prostitutes, rapists, maniacs and murderers—all the lice and scum, damned and doomed dregs of humanity, giving an advanced and ever-advancing course for young and old in all the techniques of crime and the modes of violence.

The danger of leisure, as with every other gift of God, lies in its perversion, when it leads to idleness and indolence or is given over to a round of trivial amusements and pursuits more exhausting than daily work. Karl Marx charged that religion is the opiate of the masses. Much more to the point is the contention that the real opiate of the masses is leisure. The problem is no longer to reduce labor in the interest of leisure; it is to get people to recognize that the art of using leisure well is a great part of the art of living, and that if they give it only casual attention or none at all, if they do no more than pass time or kill it, their days will be spent quite literally in shallows and in miseries. Bertrand Russell's comment gets at the dimension of the problem: "To be able to fill leisure intelligently is the last product of civilization." The last product of civilization, and surely a major concern of a Christian, for the right use of time, as of money, depends upon the belief held by the spender of the meaning and purpose of life, and is bound up with the basic questions: What is man? What is he here for? Whither is he bound?

At this level of discussion, leisure and work should be thought of together. In a well-ordered life they blend harmoniously. We shall not make the best use of our leisure if we are not making the best use of our work. The obverse of the sin of overwork is the sin of sloth, and the consequences of each are strikingly similar. Work is not, primarily, what one does to live, but what one lives to do. To be enjoyable, leisure presupposes hard and honest effort. There is solid satisfaction in relaxation *after* steady, sustained application to a task. No one can be really happy as a drone, and the enjoyment of leisure comes as the aftermath and reward of faithful toil. Home from his vacation, a man told a fellow workman that he was "back to the curse of Adam." He was thinking of the words in Genesis: "In the sweat of your face you shall eat bread." The old, primitive view was that work, being laborious, was evil and a punishment. For many today, the theological presuppositions out of the reckoning, it is a disagreeable necessity; a drudgery to be escaped from, not a discipline to be welcomed and a service to be rendered; a means of earning a living, with life beginning when the door of the office, shop, or factory closes behind them. For others, work is an opportunity for service and self-fulfillment. Their work and their life are one thing; if they were cut off from their work they would feel that they were cut off from the best part of life. For some, leisure is an escape; for others, it is a refreshment with a view to the resumption of their work and to its finer performance.

Bishop Hensley Henson, addressing a meeting of miners in his diocese, said that he worked at least sixteen hours a day and asked for nothing better. The comment of one of the miners in the audience was: "If I were a bishop I would work sixteen hours a day too, but eight hours a day of my kind of work is quite enough for anybody." Those of us whose work is congenial and full of interest, so that we feel we should pay for the privilege of engaging in it rather than be paid, ought to remember how much of the work done in the world is monotonous, meaningless, and stultifying. It affords the worker neither pride nor satisfaction; it deadens his mind and has an injurious effect on his moral as well as his mental character; it leaves no antidote for the deep boredom of his life except cheap and trivial pleasures. Wherever society is ordered more with an eye to money-making than to human welfare, wherever workers have no interest and no creative joy or pride in their work but inwardly rebel because it is endlessly repetitious, tedious and noncreative, we must not be surprised if we get intractable moral problems: low taste, mediocrity of character, intemperance, gambling, vice. People turn to the race track, the tavern, or sexual escapades to forget the dreariness and boredom of their everyday existence.

Dr. Samuel Johnson said long ago: "The reason why a man drinks is that he is not interesting enough to himself to pass his leisure time without it." That goes, also, for addiction to that "monstrous box," television. The addicts are responsible for their abuse of leisure, but even more so is the social system that has conditioned them. When one considers the nature of the work some are asked to do, the conditions under which they work, the homes to which they go at the end of the day, is it to be expected that they will read Shakespeare, sit down at the piano and play the *Moonlight Sonata,* prefer culture to slapstick comedy on television? They say in the Bowery that to get drunk is the quickest way out of New York City.

The problem of leisure is bound up with the problem of work. The nature of the one affects the appetite for the other. Work should make men as well as things. A very great deal has been done to ameliorate conditions, but we need to go on remodeling the social system so that jobs which do not offer an interesting and useful life and an opportunity for the development of character are reduced to a minimum. We should be seeking constantly for techniques whereby far more men and women than at present can achieve in their working lives the reality of self-expression, and exercise to the full their natural, God-given powers. This sort of thing may not be said often in churches, but it needs to be said. If more were said about it, might not the artisan class be less detached from the churches? Conditions being what they are, isn't it what Christ would say? Surely the aim of Christian citizens ought to be to organize society so that all work increases human well-being and so that workers feel they are carrying out some part of God's good purpose for the world.

I have been stating the case in broad and general terms. Now I want to offer a bill of particulars. We are going to have more and still more leisure. We should budget it as carefully as we do our money if we are to become the sort of persons God would have us be.

Some of it should be given to *rest*. We must sleep in order to renew ourselves after the physical and nervous fatigue of the day. There are no hard and fast rules about this. Each of us must discover how much or how little he requires. Edison got past with four hours. As we grow older, the majority of us need less than the eight hours that once constituted a minimum. Perhaps all that has to be insisted upon is that for the Christian, sloth is one of the seven deadly sins.

Some of our leisure should be given to *relaxation*. There is sound common sense in "Sometimes I sits and thinks and sometimes I just sits." A colleague once found the statesman Lord Asquith absorbed in reading a popular periodical. Asked what he was reading, Asquith was somewhat embarrassed. "As a matter of fact," he said, "it's a story called *Archie and the Sausage-chappie*." Then, more confidently, he added: "It's very good; it's by P. G. Wodehouse." No defense of Asquith's light reading is called for. The bigger the job a man has, the more necessary it is for him to relax. It must be remembered, though, that relaxation is subject to what the economists call the "Law of Diminishing Returns." Great benefit is derived from a couple of hours of taking it easy; but ten times as much is not derived from twenty hours. Relaxation is good medicine, in small doses.

Some of our leisure should be given to *self-improvement*. Does that suggest Benjamin Franklin? Perhaps we have reacted too unsympathetically against Benjamin Franklin's techniques for ordering the day. We are too slack, too self-indulgent. Most of us, for example, should make a habit of reading more discriminatingly than we do. Balzac, after spending an evening with friends who talked about everything in general and nothing of consequence, went to his study when he got home, took off his coat, rubbed his hands, and with his eye on the works of the masters on his shelves, said, "Now for some real people." The ancient Greeks could teach us all a lesson in this matter. They elevated leisure into a national art. It was regarded as essential to good citizenship. Games, festivals, and dramatic performances all formed a part of what was really organized leisure. For men like Socrates and Plato, Pericles and Demosthenes, the things of supreme worth were not money-making and status-seeking, but the development of the body, the cultivation of the mind, the growth of the soul.

Some of our leisure should be given to *voluntary service*. We ought to have an avocation as well as a vocation. We ought to involve ourselves in causes, movements, other peoples' troubles. Abilities vary, for God made us different that we might supply each other's needs, but opportunities for service are always close at hand—in the home, the church, the community. Your work from Monday to Friday is the service you render the community in return for which you are paid, though the pay is probably not your only or main reason for performing it. Voluntary service is the time, energy, and skill you freely give because you believe that "bearing one another's burdens" is the law of Christ.

Finally, some of our leisure should be given to *worship*. Thoreau, who has so much to say that our generation needs to hear, wrote, "He has true leisure who has time to improve his soul's estate." This was why in the Divine economy a whole day in every week was set apart for rest and worship. It was to be a holy day, not a holiday. We have built a lopsided civilization, for while leisure has increased, worship has diminished. Rest, relaxation, recreation, volunteer service, worship —all make their contributions to the good life. All are important, but if we have 120 hours a week out of 168 to be shared among them, is one hour enough for God?

Consider what happens in worship. As William Temple stated the case, the conscience is quickened by the holiness of God, the mind is fed with the truth of God, the imagination is purged by the beauty of God, the heart is opened to the love of God, the will is devoted to the purpose of God. Is one hour a week enough for that?

A minister was asked to call on an old man who was dying and who was afraid of death. As tenderly as he knew how, he spoke to him about God and Christ and the salvation of his soul. Bitterly and brokenly the old man complained: "I have led a very busy life. I have never had time for that sort of thing." *But he had had four thousand Sundays.*

XIX

The Struggle for Power:
A Problem of Our Time

The disciples James and John once went to Jesus and indicated that they had a request to make which they would like Him to grant. Jesus asked what they wanted Him to do for them and was told it was their wish, when He came into His Kingdom, to be allowed to sit, one on His right hand and the other on His left. It was an impudent, presumptuous, selfish request, devoid of delicacy, heedless of wounding the susceptibilities of others, but a request true to human nature as it reveals itself in every age. Influence peddling is an old and well-established business. Self-seeking and place-hunting have been common from generation to generation. Even Jesus had associates who would have made Him the tool of their egoism and ambition and who somehow persuaded themselves—how little they knew Him!—that He would yield to mere solicitation and bestow office as a favor, not because of fitness for it.

The love of power is deep-seated in human nature. It is one of the most elemental and insatiable of all human urges. Said Sancho Panza: "So sweet a thing is it to command, though it be only a flock of sheep." Adler, the psychologist, thought that the desire for power was the dominant desire in man. If it is not *the* dominant desire it is certainly one of them. There is hardly a corner of the world where little Napoleons are not competing for prestige and status, looking about them restlessly and asking, "Who is bigger?" "Who is richer?" "Who has more?"

What will men not do to be able to impose their will on others, to be head of something—a shop, an industry, a city,

135

a church? And the bigger the organization the more gratify-
ing it is to be in the place of power.

> Why, then the world's mine oyster,
> Which I with sword will open.

For this, men will work themselves into ill-health, will sacrifice leisure and pleasure, are never at ease until they can tell
someone what to do, until they feel nobody can tell *them*
"where to get off." How many marriages have been wrecked
by nothing else than this primitive craving to command and
to be obeyed? How many young people have risen in rebellion
against a childhood lived in the grip of a dictator in the home?
I think of a woman who said grimly and with an irony
touched with bitterness as though she had been cheated of
something, "Father always allowed us to have *his* own way."

The love of power and the struggle for it are seen even more
in the wider relationships of life, in the tension between class
and class, between nation and nation. First there is the struggle to gain power, and then the struggle to keep it. Nowadays
when nations go to war they are at pains to emphasize that
they are not bent on conquest. The war, they say, is a defensive war, not an offensive one. Generally what they are de-
fending is power already secured; their object is to preserve
the balance of power. With the world in a state of turmoil and
unrest, anybody can see that the balance of power is a very
precarious thing. Even if they strive to make the balance stable
by long-term treaties it may be upset at any moment, as it has
been upset in Asia, by an intense and insurgent nationalism.
This is what makes it so difficult for the United Nations to
function effectively. It calls in the general interest for a considerable surrender of national power, of sovereign rights. But
what nation, large or small, is disposed to surrender power?
There is no government in the world which would not be im-
mediately ousted from office by the political forces behind it if
it were to surrender any considerable proportion of its power
and prestige. No party government dare do such a thing.

Here, in the struggle for power, and in the convulsive shift in its distribution, is a major problem of our time. Arnold Toynbee says that before 1914 the West European middle class really ran the world. There has been a tremendous transfer of power since then. Two global wars have weakened Europe as a factor in the world, have led to a breaking down of the authority of all the empires that once maintained law and order in most of Asia and Africa, have fed the flames of nationalism among subject peoples everywhere, have contributed to the immense and spectacular expansion of the influence and might of Russia and the United States. The problem of the survival of civilization rests on the razoredge of power politics. What makes the people of America, who today stand on a pinnacle of power and wealth, apprehensive, more apprehensive perhaps than any other people, is the fear that what has happened to other nations may happen to America, that it may have to reckon with a long, drawn-out decline, culminating in the diminished stature which has been the lot of one mighty empire after another since the days of the Babylonians and the Caesars. It is Toynbee who points out that as soon as a nation becomes imperial, the seeds of disintegration are at work in it.

The apprehension has not been eased by the discovery and exploitation of nuclear energy. Ours is the dilemma of Frankenstein. How are we to avoid being destroyed by powers which we have ourselves brought into existence? In recent years the amount of power in the world has undergone a staggering increase. It is not simply power over nature; it is power over persons, the power of some men over other men and of some nations over other nations. The question at issue is whether those who hold power will recognize any moral standards as ultimate and binding on them, as having a God-given authority superior to their own interests and ambitions.

The problem of power is a moral problem. The Bible grapples with it on page after page. Jesus had a great deal to say about it. Observe His reply to the request of James and John for recognition when He came into His Kingdom:

You are aware how those who are regarded as rulers among the Gentiles lord it over them, and their great men make them feel their authority; but it is not to be so among you. No, whoever desires to be great among you must be your servant; and whoever desires to be first among you must be the bondslave of all. The Son of Man did not come to be served but to serve and to give his life a ransom for many.

What a reversal of current standards!

Observe Jesus' reply to Pilate when the Roman governor, losing patience with his prisoner, exclaimed: "You will not speak to me? Do you not know that I have power to release you, and power to crucify you?" "You would have no power over me," Jesus replied, "unless it had been given you from above." Another reversal of generally accepted standards! The power a man exercises is not his own, to be loved or used for its own sake. It is *delegated* power and comes from God. He has it as a sacred trust. He has it to do justice with it. The greater the power the more blameworthy the misuse of it. If he misuses it, he is a usurper. If he misuses it, it will evaporate. Striking teaching, and borne out by the facts of history. Think of the usurpers who have set themselves to build up empires on naked power, on sheer force. Think of Hitler, for a time almost like a Colossus bestriding the world. But only for a time. Such a tyranny over life and liberty could not in the nature of things, in God's world, last for long. It is history which makes it ridiculous to say, "Blessed are the Caesars, the Napoleons, the Stalins: for they shall inherit the earth."

The struggle for power is a major problem of our time, and about it the Christian religion has indeed much to say. *It warns us that power is a temptation to men and nations,* that both are most vulnerable, not where they are weak but where they are strong, that if the world has been sown with the seed of tears it has time and again been because of strong men loving power for its own sake and using it ruthlessly to their own advantage. About this, Viscount Grey, minister of Foreign Affairs in Britain for many years, wrote: "I think one of the saddest things, as you reflect on the history of the world, is the mischief which has been done, the opportunities which have been missed, by men with great powers in great places being unable to forget themselves."

It warns us that power corrupts character. The pursuit of it, as the case of James and John plainly shows, is by its nature a quarrelsome occupation. It leads to provocation and cruelty. The strong, as they climb to power, are apt not only to be regardless of the weak but to trample on them. It leads to presumption and pride. Give a man power and still more power, and unless he is a quite exceptional person, it will go to his head. It will make him assertive and arrogant, accustomed to do as he pleases, indignant if his will is resisted. He will be tempted to forget that people matter and should always be treated with respect, never as a means to an end. This is why in a democracy, government exists primarily as a check on the unprincipled exercise of power. Among us, power, just because of what it does to men, is not permitted to go uncriticized or uncurbed or to become absolute. Under a totalitarian regime things are different. Drunk with power, there are rulers prepared to liquidate or sterilize or "condition" whole groups of people. "You cannot make omelets," they say, "without breaking eggs." Consider the effect of such a cold-blooded attitude on the individual who adopts it—how he struts, how hard and insensitive he becomes, how pathetically small and childish he is. Dickens has a character, Jonas Chuzzlewit, who, when he was appointed a director of a swindling company, exulted over the prospect of "making a swingeing profit and having a lot of chaps to order about." Jonas Chuzzlewit is one of Dickens' most mean-minded villains. There is something sacrilegious as well as demoralizing in deriving satisfaction from having a lot of chaps to order about. It takes its toll on character. It makes men petty, officious, overbearing, offensive. "Power," said Lord Acton, and as a historian he must have schooled himself to avoid generalizations, "corrupts; absolute power corrupts absolutely."

Moreover, though men and nations crave power, and strug-

gle for it, there is something greater and in the long run far
more enduring. There is a philosophy of life that builds its
trust on deeper things. There have always been great souls
unintimidated by worldly power: Nathan confronting David,
Martin Luther at the Diet of Worms, Edith Cavell facing a
firing squad, Jesus Christ before Pilate. Why were they unintimidated? Because they believed that the world's foundations are spiritual and that force is powerless to establish
falsehood or to thwart the realization of the Divine purpose.
This is God's world. The issues of destiny are not settled by
the biggest battalions. So William James wrote:

> I am against bigness and greatness in all their forms, and with the
> invisible molecular moral forces that work from individual to indi-
> vidual, stealing in through the crannies of the world like so many soft
> rootlets, or like the capillary oozing of water, and yet rending the
> hardest monuments of man's pride, if you give them time.

There is something deeper and in the long run more enduring than the power men and nations crave. Jesus shows us
what it is. For Him nobody is great who is not humble. A real
person, he says, is not self-assertive. He does not push or drive
or desire to dominate. He believes in the power of love to overcome hate, and relies more on gentleness than on force. He
is free from pride and arrogance because he recognizes his
dependence on a Power higher than any earthly power. This
is not popular doctrine; it is neither generally accepted nor
generally practiced; but in our best moments we know that
it is true and that if it were generally practiced the world
would be an infinitely happier place.

Reading a sports column some years ago, I came across this
cameo:

> The old Durocher was brash, arrogant, noisy, impetuous, impatient,
> argumentative, pitiless and utterly contemptuous of the other fellow.
> His philosophy was wrapped up in his one scathing description of Mel
> Ott. "Nice guys finish last," barked The Lip, never dreaming that
> some day he himself would change into a nice guy and finish first.
> . . . The old Durocher would have been insufferable in unexpected

victory. The new one accepted the most magnificent triumph of his checkered career with complete humility. He hardly raised his voice. He didn't crow. He took no credit. "The boys did it themselves. I merely waved them home from the third base coaching box," he said. He meant it, too. Every word of it. . . . When Willie Mays first joined the Giants he made one hit in his first twenty-six times at bat. The old Durocher would have banished him mercilessly to his doghouse. But when the weeping 20-year-old boy came to his manager and begged that he be benched before he hurt the team, the new Durocher draped a fatherly arm about the youngster's shoulders. . . . "Don't worry, son," he said understandingly, "you're my center fielder even if you don't get another hit all season." . . . The shiny-eyed Mays strode from Leo's office with buoyant step and promptly began to hit like crazy.

For Jesus, moreover, nobody can be great whose life is not construed in terms of service. "If any one would be first he must be last of all and servant of all." The highest self-realization is achieved through self-renunciation. Earlier we noted that power can be a temptation; it can also provide an opportunity, and what an opportunity. When power is dedicated not to selfish ends but to the common good, it can be a beneficent thing. When it seeks not to be served but to serve, a saving element enters into life and redeems it from pettiness and vulgarity. This is not visionary idealism. This is a law of life corroborated by the facts of history. The great souls of the earth are never browbeating, hectoring, contentious; they are the men and women whose motto is the motto of the British Royal House: "I serve."

The struggle for power is a problem of our time. What can we do about it? Because of the colossal scale of the influences at work we may feel that there is little we can do. Because the problems are so vast we may think there is no place where we can take hold with any effectiveness. There is something we can do. We can make our lives count. We can help set the world right by being set right ourselves. We can live for the things that are greater and more enduring than power. We can refuse to push and drive and dominate. We can build our trust on deeper things. We can rely not on push and pull but on the spiritual influences at once in operation wherever men seek to be selfless and to dedicate their strength to the service of mankind. Others may call this sentimental idealism. We cannot, if we profess and call ourselves followers of Him who said, "If any man would come after me, let him deny himself and take up his cross daily and follow me."

XX

Jesus and Status Seeking

To judge accurately the character of a culture we must be familiar with the type of man it holds up for its ideal. The ideal of the Greeks was the perfectly proportioned personality, the personality that had achieved a rounded completeness. The ideal of the Romans was the soldier, embodying the Stoic virtues of discipline and courage. Coming closer to our own time, the ideal of Hitler and his henchmen was the superman, dominating and regimenting supposedly lesser breeds.

What type of man does our culture hold up for its ideal? The successful man, the man who outstrips his fellows and becomes wealthy, prominent, powerful. In America and the West generally, we think of life as a pyramid, with the successful at the peak and the ambitious striving to achieve a position where there are fewer equals and more and more subordinates. Young people setting out in the morning for school, in their freshman year at college, making a start in business, are exhorted by their parents and elders to take "Excelsior" for their motto and to remember that there is plenty of room at the top.

A few days after publication, Vance Packard's book, *The Status Seekers,* became a best seller. This is a significant fact, for best sellers are indicative of a country's trends and tastes— *Lady Chatterley's Lover* no less than *The Status Seekers.* Packard's thesis is that any number can play the status-seeking game and that in every walk of life people seem to be trying it, as can be seen in their homes, furniture, automobiles, clubs, all status symbols and clues to their social rank. He points out that advertisements of luxury items in newspapers and magazines are aimed at such characteristics as cupidity, ostentation, snobbery. He has little difficulty in showing that churches are no exception to the general trend. Materialistic scales of value are accepted, and success measured by the size of buildings, the amount of the annual budget, the number of members on the church roll.

Jesus had a great deal to say about status seeking. Sometimes in His comments He was gently ironical. Observing how prestige conscious the average person was, how bent on getting recognition, how hurt in his dignity when recognition was denied him, He said—surely with a smile—poking fun at human vanity: "When anyone invites you to a banquet never occupy the best place, in case a more distinguished guest than yourself has been invited; then the host will tell you, 'Make room for him,' and you will proceed in shame to take the lowest place. No, when you are invited, go and occupy the lowest place, so that when your host comes in he will tell you, 'Move higher up, my friend.' Then you will be honored before your fellow guests." Gentle irony! Pettiness is often better laughed at—gently—than scolded.

At other times the note sounded was sterner. With *churchmen* who were status seekers, basking in the limelight, never so happy as when fawned on and adulated, more concerned with outward appearance than inner character, Jesus had no patience. "Beware of the scribes, who like to go about in long robes, and to have salutations in the market places and the best seats in the synagogues and the places of honor at feasts, who devour widows' houses and for a pretense make long prayers. They will receive the greater condemnation." No period piece that! Accurate in observation and detail, it fits our status-seeking generation. The long robes—an academic community knows all about their use as status symbols. Who was it, impishly mocking academic vanity, suggested that B.D. stands for Barely Dumb, D.D. for Definitely Dumb, Ph.D. for Phenomenally Dumb? The salutations—"How are you, Doctor?" "You never looked better, Madam President." "It is a pleasure to know you, Senator." The best seats, the places of honor—at a public meeting I once saw a man—he was in his sixties and the president of an organization—stalk in high dudgeon from the platform when told that his seat was not in the front row but in the second. And there was the case of the woman who nearly wept her eyes out because her name had been inadvertently omitted from the list of bazaar stallholders.

Most of the time, what Jesus had to say about status seeking was revolutionary. To this day, humanity has failed to take the measure of His teaching, has certainly failed to act upon it. He reverses universally accepted standards and values, flatly contradicts them, challenges what we take for granted, cuts across pride of place and race and power. A generation is growing up that is ignorant of the Bible. In our fiercely competitive culture, with its intensified social stratification and its passion for wealth and prestige, what must be the reaction of thoughtful young folk encountering for the first time these sayings of Christ: "You know that the rulers of the Gentiles lord it over them, and their great men exercise authority over them. It shall not be so among you; but whoever would be great among you must be your servant, and whoever would be first among you must be slave of all." Again, "If any one would be first, he must be last of all and servant of all." And again, "But many that are first will be last, and the last first." Isn't that in stark contrast to the spirit of the age? What is needed to get to the top, we are told, is an assertive quality, a clever, calculating mind, feelings not too sensitive to the misfortunes of others, plenty of self-confidence and something of a flair for self-advertisement.

What gives weight to these sayings of Jesus is His character, His deeds, His life. He was utterly indifferent to any man's economic status. He had the aristocracy of mind which treats the rich and the poor alike. He attached no importance to social registers. He was not born with a silver spoon in His mouth. He grew up in a poor home, was a carpenter, washed the feet of His disciples, rode on a donkey, died at the last on a Cross. It was this that left those who knew Him best awestruck—that He made Himself of no reputation, took upon

Him the form of a servant, was made in the likeness of man, and being found in fashion as a man humbled Himself and became obedient unto death, even the death of the Cross. And yet all through His life He dwarfed everyone around Him, in moral stature towered head and shoulders above all His contemporaries, so that if we know anything about Caesar Augustus and Caiaphas, Herod and Pilate, it is because of their association with Him. He is still without rival or peer. Alongside of Him the great ones of the earth sink into insignificance.

In all this there is one consideration to bear in mind. Never suppose that Jesus forbade His followers to seek greatness. On the contrary, day after day He stressed their God-given status, their latent possibilities, their unique worth and value. To be sure, He made much of the virtue of humility, but of all the Christian virtues it has been the most misunderstood. It is constantly confused with self-disparagement, though it would not have occurred to Jesus to link humility with nonentity, or meekness with mediocrity. William Beebe, the naturalist, made many visits to the home of Theodore Roosevelt, himself something of a naturalist. After an evening's talk the two men would go out-of-doors, gaze up at the sky, and see who first could detect the faint spot of light-mist beyond the lower left-hand corner of the Great Square of Pegasus, and then one or the other would recite: "That is the Spiral Galaxy in Andromeda. It is as large as our Milky Way. It is one of a hundred million galaxies. It is 750,000 light-years away. It consists of one hundred billion suns, each larger than our sun." Whereupon, Beebe reports, Roosevelt would grin at him and say: "Now I think we are small enough. Let's go to bed." A salutary exercise for all status seekers! The thing that impresses one, however, is that it was never human littleness that Jesus stressed but human grandeur. "You are the salt of the earth." "You are the light of the world." "You, therefore, must be perfect, as your heavenly Father is perfect." Those striking sayings were addressed to fishermen and small-town business men. In the *Te Deum* they are hailed as "the glorious company of the Apostles," but to their Roman overlords they were a bunch of nobodies. You yourself, meeting them on the street, might not have looked twice at any of them.

Jesus never forbade His followers to seek greatness. It is right to seek it, but it should be real greatness. The qualities esteemed among us—energy, initiative, ambition, high-grade ability—are splendid qualities, with this proviso: everything depends on the ends they are made to serve and the uses to which they are put. In a self-seeking person—Joe Lampton in the novel *Room at the Top,* scheming and elbowing his way up life's ladder—they can be terribly mercenary and predatory. When so exploited they may yield wealth, prestige, success of a sort, but not real greatness. Be clear as to what Jesus says about this vital matter. You want to excel. You are ambitious. You propose to make something of your life. This He approves and applauds. This, if you are a Christian, you should and must do. Only be very sure about one thing: the nature of your ambition, the character of the success you seek, what you are really after.

Here the challenge of Jesus is searching. For example, He wants to know *where in our life plan God comes in.* Do we think ourselves self-sufficient? Do we propose through youth, the middle years, old age, to go it alone, generating our own power, making our own rules, subordinating things and people to our own purposes and designs, out for all we can get? Or do we recognize what for the Master was the beginning and the end of everything, our dependence on God, our daily need of Him, our subjecthood, the fact that we owe Him obedience as our liege Lord and are here to live our lives not as we please but in conformity with His standards and laws? Despite its churchgoing, ours is a secular, unspiritual culture. Great numbers of people, their names on church rolls, think, speak, and act in almost complete independence of God, as though He did not exist. For Jesus, so conscious of God, so devoted to God, so obedient to God, this *faithlessness* was *the* tragedy of human existence. It explained the fears and frustrations of men and women. It was a prime factor in the undermining of character and integrity. It led to shallow, superficial living—as Elizabeth Fry said about her early, indolent, self-indulgent years, "all outside and no inside," the world gained but the soul lost. For Jesus there could be no real greatness apart from God, its ultimate source.

This has special relevance for those who are on the threshold of their careers. America is a land of almost limitless opportunity. If you will work hard and long, if you will develop and discipline your native powers, you can command success. What others have done you can do. What others have done you can do better. But in all your working and planning, if you aspire after true status and want to avoid hollowness and disillusionment, make now and keep always a place for God, be ever mindful of your Maker and Master and of the recognition and obedience which are His due.

First what we owe to God, *then what we owe to our fellows.* According to Jesus, greatness is to be judged by one criterion —service. It is here particularly that He reverses generally accepted standards. To be prominent in the world's eye, to be talked about, to figure in the daily press, to be served, courted, admired—this for multitudes is greatness. Not so with Jesus. It was dedication, not rank that He cared about. In His eyes the badge of nobility was not prerogative but usefulness. Somebody has said that the only distinction He recognized was a Distinguished Service Cross. He never asked about any man: How does he rate? What is he worth? What He wanted to know was: Does he deny himself? Is he sensitive to human needs? Over and over again His counsel to His hearers was: Don't let your life revolve around your interests and ambitions; escape from the prison of self; lose yourself in a cause bigger than yourself.

He was not unique, of course, in offering such counsel. In ancient Greece, Menander gave the same advice. "This is life," he wrote, "not to live for self." Another of the ancients, Plutarch, said about his work: "This is done, not for myself, but for my country." Such patriotism gives stability and durability to a nation. Why do we hail as essentially great a man like Schweitzer, Schweitzer who at once fascinated *and* rebuked the well-fed, flabby, comfortable all over the world? Whether we realize it or not, we are applying the criterion of Jesus. No one has achieved stature who has not felt in some degree that his life was not his own to do with as he pleased, but belonged to God and his fellows, and that what God had given him in native ability and talent was given for mankind.

Once Goethe wrote confidingly to a friend: "The desire to raise the pyramid of my existence, the base of which is laid already, as high as possible into the air absorbs every other desire and will scarce consent to quit me." An unchristian ambition but strong in human nature. *How are we to reverse in ourselves the stream of interest in self and status?* How are we to get out of our own light, give up self-indulgence and self-seeking, and become expendable? By keeping before us morning and evening the example of the Master. In Him we see love to God as the inspiration of life, and love to men as the incentive to self-effacing service. For those who are bent on achieving worldly status, the Cross on which Jesus died must be of all symbols in the world the most unintelligible— a stone of stumbling and a rock of offense. Planning and pursuing your career, do you ever pause to ponder Christ's Cross?

And now as a sort of tailpiece, this story. A man dreamed he visited a celestial museum. No crowns or scepters were there, no miters or thrones, no Pope's rings nor even Martin Luther's inkpot. A handful of thorns was there, a seamless robe, a cup of cold water. "Have you a towel and basin?" the man asked. "No," said the guardian angel. "You see, they are in perpetual use." The man knew then that he was in the Holy City.

XXI

Am I My Brother's Keeper?

Familiar even to casual readers of the Bible is the question put by God to Cain, "Where is Abel your brother?" and the reply, "I do not know; am I my brother's keeper?" That flustered, evasive retort to a probing question has gone echoing down the centuries. It makes an indelible impression on the memory because in a few vivid words it sums up an attitude to which people everywhere are prone. Cain stands for all time as the prototype of the selfish individualist who disowns responsibility, ignores obligations, lacks even a semblance of social instinct. The fate that befell him is meant to serve as a grim warning. A man accursed, dwelling East of Eden, which brings to mind John Steinbeck's novel of that title, he became a fugitive and a wanderer in the earth. There could hardly be a sadder cry than his: "My punishment is greater than I can bear."

On the positive side, Cain's story is a reminder that all of us who walk the good earth are children of God and of one flesh and blood. Life is not something individual, to be shaped solely according to individual needs. On the biblical view at any rate, man is what he is only as a member of the great family of God. The basis of society, the cement which holds it together and without which it must disintegrate, is the obligation which men and nations owe to one another. No man should try to be a law to himself; no nation should. Each should care for all, and all for each. We cannot get along without the assistance of others. Our interdependence is one of the most encompassing facts of life. Stressed throughout the Bible, it is the key to the religion of the Bible, to the conception of justice, to the discernment of right from wrong.

This has been true at every stage of civilization; it is more than ever self-evident in our time. We have lived to see the continents bridged and the world become a compact community. In the Jet Age, Britain is, so to speak, two doors away, Russia across the road, China in the next street. Everybody knows everybody else's business. We can overhear one another talking. Propinquity has accentuated our interdependence. To a degree Paul never dreamed of, no nation lives to itself or dies to itself. Every day it is becoming more and more apparent that if we do not learn to live together, we will die together.

We are so interrelated that without intending it we serve one another. In a Rockefeller Foundation report issued in wartime, Dr. Raymond Fosdick wrote:

An American soldier wounded on a battlefield in the Far East owes his life to the Japanese scientist, Kitasato, who isolated the bacillus of tetanus. A Russian soldier saved by a blood transfusion is indebted to Landsteiner, an Austrian. A German soldier is shielded from typhoid fever with the help of a Russian, Metchnikoff. A Dutch marine in the East Indies is protected from malaria because of the experiments of an Italian, Grassi; while a British aviator in North Africa escapes death from surgical infection because a Frenchman, Pasteur, and a German, Koch, elaborated a new technique. Our children are guarded from diphtheria by what a Japanese and a German did; they are protected from smallpox by an Englishman's work; they are saved from rabies because of a Frenchman; they are cured of pellagra through the researches of an Austrian. From birth to death they are surrounded by an invisible host—the spirits of men who never thought in terms of flags or boundary lines and who never served a lesser loyalty than the welfare of mankind.

With that the situation, provincialism is out of date. No longer is it the case that "Oh, East is East, and West is West, and never the twain shall meet." A human interest item illustrates the point. When women in the United States began to bob their hair, twenty thousand girls were thrown out of work in China. What was the connection between bobbed hair in New York City and unemployment in Shanghai? Those Chinese girls were employed in factories making hairnets for

American women. We live in a small world. What happens in
one part of it inevitably affects life and conditions in another.
There is only one answer to the question, "Am I my brother's
keeper?" Whether we like it or not, we are.

And yet a symptom of a disease widespread in modern life
is the weakness of the sense of responsibility for what happens
in the world. Isolationism is far from dead. Provincialism
shows little sign of dying. Too many people have no interest
in matters beyond their own appetites and their immediate
senses. Too many are nonparticipating spectators in the spiritual battles of these momentous days. Too many spend their
time *watching* life, religion, politics, social undertakings, as
from a grandstand they might watch a game. They do not
identify themselves with, or involve themselves in, the issues
that are at stake. They are uncommitted. They are noncom-
batants. About Santayana, Orville Prescott wrote:

> In his old age Santayana has withdrawn farther and farther from
> the world until the long historical perspective with which he regards
> human affairs seems callous and inhuman. The infamies of Fascism
> did not perceptibly distress him; the cruelty of Communism does not
> arouse his righteous wrath. . . . Such an aloofness from the good
> fight which men must always wage against tyranny and injustice is
> understandably infuriating to men of goodwill. If it were widely
> imitated world slavery would be the inevitable end.

There is a phrase common nowadays, sometimes on the lips
even of preachers, teachers, social workers, and senators. It
is, "Why should I stick my neck out?" usually with the emphasis on the *my*. A cartoon appeared some years ago in the
New Yorker. The scene was a New York City street in broad
daylight. An ordinary, respectable citizen (who might be any
one of us) was crossing the street near an open manhole out
of which had emerged a huge octopus. It seized the man with
its tentacles and slowly dragged him down into the sewer.
He beat at it vainly with his umbrella. A crowd of passers-by
lined the sidewalk, watching what was going on with an air
of fascinated interest. But not one of them made the slightest
move to help the victim. It was not their business. They did

not know who he was. "Why should I stick my neck out?" "Am I my brother's keeper?" You may say that is exaggerated. Perhaps so; it is nevertheless too close to the facts of everyday life to leave any of us comfortable. Indeed, in New York City recently a man was knocked down and robbed at high noon with scores of people about, and not a hand was stretched out to assist him or to lay hold of and impede the robber. A woman was murdered in a parking lot one night and while her cries were heard by many people in nearby apartments, no one went to her rescue.

Does what I am saying make you think of Christ and where He put the emphasis? "You shall love your neighbor as yourself," He said. He took that commandment from its comparatively obscure place in Leviticus and set it alongside the first and greatest of the commandments, the commandment to love God. He said that it was not merely the second among many commandments but, along with the first, the center from which arise all our duties and obligations. He made it the subject of one of His most striking parables, the parable of the Good Samaritan, the whole point of the parable being that we are our brother's keeper, that we are to care as much about him as we care about ourselves (what a demand), that our concern is not to be a matter of sentiment or personal liking but of active good will, a good will carrying us beyond our family circle, our church circle, our social circle, beyond the boundaries of religion, class, and color, to serve human need wherever it exists.

The parable of the Good Samaritan is as contemporary as today's newspaper—and far more searching. Don't we see ourselves in the lawyer to whom it was addressed? Faced with the categorical imperative, "You shall love your neighbor as yourself," what did he do? He proposed a discussion. He began, or intended to begin, an argument. "Who is my neighbor?" The question was much debated at the time. What exactly did the commandment mean? Did it mean only a fellow Jew, or a fellow Jew only under certain restricted conditions? Was an extortionist like Zacchaeus a neighbor? Was a moral leper to be loved? Where did the line run? Jesus, it was common knowledge, kept strange company, was often seen with collaborators and prostitutes. How would He define a neighbor? The demand was for action, but the lawyer wanted to talk rather than to act. Aren't we like him? The world around us is full of desperate and clamant need, but instead of getting to work, tackling specific situations, *we debate the problems they present, set up committees to examine them, pass resolutions on how to deal with them.* There may be right under our eyes conditions crying out for action, but first a strategy has to be devised; they must be the subject of a survey. This postpones action, and when the findings bring out what any discriminating observer already knew were the facts, as like as not a study of the *implications* of the survey will be recommended, and take up further time. Talk, talk, talk, and all the while what is called for is involvement, self-identification, getting down to business. A committee, a wag once quipped, keeps minutes and wastes hours.

When the lawyer asked, "Who is my neighbor?" Jesus answered, "A man was going down from Jerusalem to Jericho. . . ." For generalities were substituted specifics. The point should not be lost on us. We can be enthusiastic about humanity—the victims of apartheid in South Africa, the hungry millions in the East, the population explosion and its implications—but do nothing personal and practical for those around us who require help. We can go wrong by taking so wide a view of our responsibilities that we fail to come to grips with obligations on our doorstep. An old man past looking after himself is never just a sad example of age and infirmity needing community-service care. He is a person, craving companionship and sympathy, craving even more the assurance that someone really cares for him *as a person* and is not just doing what has to be done for a very sad case, Case 232. The thing one keeps coming back to in Jesus is His concern and affection for people, the time He gave to them, the way in which He made them feel that they mattered and were needed and loved. And not just nice people, the congenial ones, the grateful ones, the moneyed ones, but the people who were hard to like, the difficult ones, the ones with body odor, the bad ones, the lost ones. Where we generalize He particularized. *He never spoke of humanity but of "your brethren."*

Do we not see ourselves in the priest and the Levite in the parable? Let us face the facts. We avert our eyes from the needs of our fellow men and from the demands their needs make on us. Our lives are full of evasions. We don't want to get mixed up in unpleasant situations, and we are relieved if we can avoid contact with them. We pass by on the other side. Nearly all of the good that people do is done by proxy and without personal inconvenience or sacrifice. It is so much easier to write a check than to deal with human need at first hand. When George Meredith's novel *The Egoist* was published, one of his friends read it with eagerness, intending to send his congratulations. In the unlovely character of its leading figure, however, he sensed a strange likeness to himself. To the author he wrote indignantly, "It is too bad of you, Meredith—Willoughby is me!" "No," replied Meredith, "Willoughby is all of us." Egoists all of us, preoccupied with self, neglectful of others. We have not lived in the way of love or even in the way of duty. If our soul's salvation lay in our being judged as to whether we had loved our neighbor as we love ourselves, which is the point of another parable of our Lord's, the parable of the Last Judgment, we could have no assurance of standing before God or of inheriting eternal life.

Egoists all of us? No. To the general rule there are exceptions. "But a Samaritan"—to get the effect today perhaps we should say, But a Communist—"as he journeyed, came to where he was: and when he saw him, he had compassion, and went to him and bound up his wounds, pouring on oil and wine; then he set him on his own beast and brought him to an inn, and took care of him." (Such a succession of active verbs!) And European theologians charge the American churches with being activist! Would that we were far more active, socially active. Thank God for what all Good Samaritans have done: Vinoba in India, Dolci in Palermo, Schweitzer in Africa, Mellon in Haiti, Tom Dooley in Laos, Howard Rusk in New York City. Thank God for a woman like Dorothy Day, one of the great self-spending souls of our generation in whom the spirit of St. Francis of Assisi has come alive again. An American in Liberia talked with an official about Liberia's head, President Tubman. He had noted the tremendous influence that the President wielded and he asked for the secret of it. The reply he received was, "We have a saying here that if a little boy out in the bush stubs his toe, President Tubman says 'Ouch.'" Compassion, fellow feeling, self-identification, sensitivity to need, readiness to respond to it, loving one's neighbor as oneself—that is Christianity in action.

This chapter can have only one conclusion. "Go and do likewise."

XXII

The Materialism of Christianity

One of the chief foes of the Christian religion is materialism. What is materialism? It is the theory that material well-
being is the chief end of man, and that the things we can
touch, taste, see, smell, hear are the only realities. A materialistic society is one that assesses value in terms of the abundance of earthly goods. It is a society in which the goals of
living and the standards of success are mercenary and self-
regarding. It is a society in which a man's worth is measured
not by his beliefs, morals, loyalties but by the car he drives,
the clothes his wife wears, the liquor he dispenses at parties,
the clubs to which he belongs. Materialism is pursuit of the
dollar sign. A child saw a rainbow for the first time and was
impressed by its beauty and brilliance. She turned to her
mother and asked, "What is it advertising?" A sad commentary, that, on the predominantly materialistic character of
our society, though to keep the picture in perspective the remark of the child may be matched by something said by a
nurse in one of our hospitals. A visitor watching her work with
a ghastly wound commented, "I wouldn't do that for a million
dollars." "Neither would I," the nurse answered.

There is another type of materialism. We call it philosophical materialism. It maintains that there is nothing above or
beyond or outlasting the ongoing natural process of which
we form a part. Marxian Communism is a case in point. It is
a materialistic creed. The determining factor in life, it says,
is the struggle for bread, the economic factor. The only
achievement possible to men is the creation of a society on
earth free from the faults of all previous societies. It is fruitless
for us to cherish any aim or purpose in life that reaches be-

157

yond this world, for there is nothing beyond this world. There is no God, no afterlife, no salvation for us other than we ourselves can accomplish here and now. Religion is a lie, an illusion, an opiate by means of which multitudes console themselves for their sufferings and frustrations, and as such it is exploited in the interests of a ruling class. The *Communist Manifesto* says that "the parson has ever gone hand in hand with the landlord." Lenin is more emphatic. "Religion is a sort of spiritual moonshine [bad home-made liquor] in which the slaves of Capital drown . . . their demands for even any sort of human working life."

The uncompromising materialism of the Marxian Communist dispenses with religion in any shape or form. It is the officially declared and zealously propagated creed of countries containing at least a third of the population of the world. Nothing, however, could be more misleading or mistaken than to contrast a godless East with a religious West. Marxian Communism is a Western product. The atheism for which it stands is not all on the other side of the Iron Curtain. In many universities in the Western world, among faculty and students, there are those who contend that belief in God is impossible for an enlightened mind. Advocacy of the belief finds no place in the curriculum; it is neither inculcated nor expressly repudiated; what is more deadly, it is ignored. Materialism is indeed one of the chief foes of the Christian religion.

And yet the Christian religion, in the words of William Temple, is "the most avowedly materialist of all the great religions." When I say that, I am not forgetting that one of its central affirmations is that "God is Spirit, and those who worship Him must worship in spirit and truth," or that another of its fundamental propositions is that "the things that are seen are transient, but the things that are unseen are eternal." Christianity is a spiritual religion. It asserts the reality of the spiritual world and man's inability to live by bread alone, but it has a decidedly materialistic aspect. It exalts the spiritual above the material, but unlike some of the other great religions, it never ignores the material, it never minimizes its importance. On the contrary, it recognizes its place in the Divine plan and seeks its sanctification. The higher, it says, can exist only by means of the lower. The two, matter and spirit, body and soul, are interrelated and interdependent. And when we speak of higher and lower, lower means what is secondary; it does not mean something that is irremediably evil. This is nowhere made more plain than in the central affirmation of the Bible: "The Word became flesh."

Turning now to specific instances, consider how avowedly materialist Christianity is. *It maintains that the material world is the work of God;* that the Eternal Spirit whom we worship created the world of matter and is intimately connected with it; that while He made man in His own image with spirit, reason, and freedom, He rooted his life in nature and fitted him with a bodily organism sympathetic with natural forces and acting in unison with them. The writer of the Creation narrative in Genesis says that God saw everything He had made, and behold, it was very good. The prophets stress not only that God is the Lord of history, raising up leaders, controlling events, inaugurating new eras, but that it is He who sends rain on the earth and gives fertility to flocks and fields. Most of us live out of touch with nature. Our food comes to us from the factory or the bakery. We are apt to forget that

> Back of the loaf is the snowy flour,
>   And back of the flour is the mill,
> And back of the mill is the wheat and the shower,
>   And the sun and the Father's will.

The material world is a sacrament. The sea, the sky, the sunshine, the mountains—they are all the outward and visible sign of an inward and invisible Spirit. Christ bade us consider the flowers and the birds. He saw the mark of a miracle on every grain of wheat. All the way through the Bible the emphasis is the same—this world of time and sense, of sight and sound, came from God, and we were set in it by Him.

Do we really believe this? I press the question because it is a belief that has sociological and economic implications. Each harvest confronts the United States with an "economy of abundance." We take pride in our natural resources and in our modern, up-to-date implements and mechanized equipment, but where would our abundance be if there were no life in the seed and no fertility in the soil? We can sow seed, but we cannot create seed. What we speak of as our natural resources are not ours. "The earth is the Lord's and the fulness thereof." We are here to be responsible stewards of its bounty and wealth. We have no right to act irresponsibly, misusing or abusing foodstuffs, raw material, the land, the matter and energy inherent in nature. "Beware," the Bible warns us, "lest you say in your heart, 'My power and the might of my hand have gotten me this wealth.' You shall remember the Lord your God, for it is he who gives you power to get wealth." It is when this is denied, forgotten, insufficiently emphasized that men fall into a false spirituality which views the world with indifference—"'Earth is a desert drear, heaven is my home,'" as the old hymn put it—or, viewing it selfishly, exploits it to personal advantage and profit.

As further illustrating the materialist character of Christianity, consider *the significance it attaches to the human body.* There was a thinker in ancient Greece named Porphyry who was so devoted to the life of the spirit that he was ashamed of his body. Nothing could be more unchristian. The supreme revelation of God is in the taking on of human flesh by His Son. This is the culmination and crowning point of the whole sacramental view of the world. "The Word became flesh." This is why Christians think of the body as sacred. "Do you not know that your body is a temple of the Holy Spirit?" Paul asked the Corinthians. He took a high view of the body. Its care and discipline were an essential part of his personal religion. We have a proverb which says that cleanliness is next to godliness. I doubt whether Paul would have said that; he might rather have said that cleanliness is a part of godliness. He certainly did nothing to impair the functions of his body or to enfeeble its powers. He regarded the human body as sacred.

Here is another belief that has sociological implications. What it implies is that sensuality is sacrilege. Immorality defiles the soul and drives the Holy Spirit out of it. The supreme motive for continence is not consideration of the wrong done to another, grievous as that is. It is not the disciplinary motive of controlling the lower appetites, necessary as that is. It is the obligation, binding and absolute, to keep the body as well as the soul free from sin. "Shall I therefore take the members of Christ and make them members of a prostitute?" is Paul's most pointed inquiry, just as his more positive exhortation is, "I appeal to you therefore, brethren, by the mercies of God, to present your bodies as a living sacrifice, holy and acceptable to God, which is your spiritual worship."

The positive aspect of the case should be emphasized. If the body is sacred the sexual nature is not something of which men and women have any need to be ashamed. It is not compounded of guilty desires which marriage disposes of quietly and with propriety. Sex is a part of human nature which can be a source of deep fulfillment and rich fruitfulness. Because man is a spirit, the importance of marriage as a spiritual union cannot be overemphasized. But the relationship is also physical, and there is no taint attaching to it for that reason. Sex and sin are not synonymous. We talk about the world, the flesh and the Devil as though God had joined them together. God did not join them together. It is the business of Christians to divorce the world and the flesh from the Devil.

The materialist character of Christianity is also seen in the fact that *it never minimizes the physical necessities of man's existence.* It is not a purely spiritual religion. If Jesus says, "Man shall not live by bread alone," He enjoins His disciples to pray, "Give us this day our daily bread." The order of the clauses in the Lord's Prayer is illuminating. It begins with God—Thy Name, Thy Kingdom, Thy Will—then our bread, our debts, our temptations, our deliverance; and then, swinging back again, Thine is the Kingdom, the Power, the Glory. It is the order of the perfect life, and in it the next thing after God is bread.

Some of the early Church Fathers took the petition for daily bread as meaning spiritual or sacramental bread. They clean missed the materialist element in the Gospels, our Lord's concern not alone for the salvation of men's souls but for the well-being of their bodies. The Temptation shows that the problem of bread for the people was much on His mind. Again and again He assured men and women that God was concerned with their material needs—food, drink, clothes—as well as their spiritual needs. He did not isolate the material, and minister to it alone. He knew how interrelated the body and soul are, and how they react on each other. He forgave a man's sins and healed his sickness as part of one process. There is nothing new about the psychosomatic approach. Christ practiced it one thousand nine hundred years ago. But just because so many persons think of Christianity as a purely spiritual religion, and keep their religion separate and distinct from the affairs of everyday life, it must be emphasized that Christ was never indifferent to men's material needs and social condition.

Nor should His followers be indifferent. As has been said, until the cry for bread—and that includes the cry for a decent home and a wholesome environment and a just social order— is answered, there can be no rest for Christ, and no rest for the Church, and no rest for any of us who call Him Lord. It is a clamant cry for bread that sounds in our ears today. Take Asia as an example. It has the lowest per capita level of income and production in the world. Several years ago I saw the income per annum in China, per head of the population, estimated at $23, in India, $46; but for Britain the estimate was $660 and for the United States, $1,500. What an opportunity America has of demonstrating the best kind of Christian materialism. Fairly recent figures show that it contains 6 per cent of the world's area and 7 per cent of its population. It normally consumes 48 per cent of the world's coffee, 53 per cent of its tin, 56 per cent of its rubber, 72 per cent of its silk. It operates 60 per cent of the world's telephones and 80 per cent of the motor cars. It produces 70 per cent of the oil, 60 per

cent of the wheat and cotton, and 50 per cent of the copper
and pig iron output of the globe. It possesses about $11,000,-
000,000 in gold, or nearly half the world's monetary metal.
The purchasing power of its population is greater than that
of the 500,000,000 people in Europe. With such abundance,
Americans have a rare opportunity of demonstrating the finest kind of Christian materialism. ". . . I was hungry and you
gave me food, . . . I was naked and you clothed me, . . . as you
did it to one of the least of these my brethren, you did it
to me."

William Makepeace Thackeray heard that one of his neighbors, an elderly widow, was ill. He knew that she was in
straitened circumstances. Genteel poverty can be the worst
sort of poverty. What do you suppose Thackeray did? He got
a pillbox from the druggist, filled it with gold half-sovereigns
and wrote on the box, "One to be taken when required." Then
he wrapped it up and had it delivered at her door. That is
Christian materialism at its best. We cheat our consciences if
we talk about money as filthy lucre. Where the Bible places the
emphasis is on its use and abuse. Money can be a beautiful
thing. Think of what it can purchase, things that are as much
spiritual as they are material: good food and healthy homes,
education and recreation, churches and hospitals and neigh-
borhood centers and mission stations. With it we can serve
God and advance His Kingdom. We are stewards of it and
answerable to Him for the use we make of it. Here, in the
importance it attaches to money, is one more illustration of
the materialism of Christianity.

And now to sum up. The Christian religion is not a separate
province, a particular area of life to be labeled spiritual as
over against what is secular or material. It is all of life looked
at with the eyes of Christ and lived out in the spirit of Christ.
A man cannot be a Christian inside the church fellowship,
and something else outside. The life of the true Christian is
all of one piece. He does not share in Christian worship and
then go out into the world to deal selfishly or irresponsibly
with money or goods, nor cruelly or callously with people. "If

Holy Communion does not lead to honest commerce, it fails of its fruit, and by their fruits ye shall know them." God is our King, Christ is our Lord, not only when we are at worship and prayer but also in whatever we are doing and wherever and whenever we are doing it. Within one living person Christ united in Himself both flesh and spirit. This is what we must seek to be—a living unity of flesh and spirit. It may have been of this that Browning was thinking when he wrote:

> Let us not always say,
> "Spite of this flesh to-day
> I strove, made head, gained ground upon the whole!"
> As the bird wings and sings.
> Let us cry, "All good things
> Are ours, nor soul helps flesh more, now, than flesh helps soul!"

It was certainly of the living unity of body and spirit that Paul was thinking when he wrote, ". . . therefore glorify God in your body, and in your spirit, which are God's."

Sources

Page Line

5 2   Bertrand Russell, *A Free Man's Worship* (Mosher, 1927), p. 6.

   11–14 Hugh Walpole, *Vanessa* (Doubleday, 1933), p. 80.

   15–21 James B. Pratt, *The Religious Consciousness* (Macmillan, 1927), p. 217.

6 23 ff. John Gillespie Magee, Jr., "High Flight," in the *New York Herald Tribune*, Feb. 8, 1942.

9 13–14 Wordsworth, "Prelude" VI.

   18–19 Jer. 10:23, K.J.V.

13 20 ff. Dorothy Sayers, *Creed or Chaos?* (Harcourt, Brace, 1949), pp. 28, 29.

16 24   William Wordsworth, "Tintern Abbey."

19 3–6   George Matheson, "Gather us in, thou Love that fillest all," in *Hymns for the Living Age* (Century, 1923), No. 392, stanza 2.

22 22–24 E. Stanley Jones, *Christ at the Round Table* (Hodder and Stoughton, 1928), p. 288.

25 4–5   Job 2:9.

   20–25 Quoted in T. H. Darlow, *Life and Letters of William Robertson Nicoll* (Hodder and Stoughton, 1925), p. 171.

27 12–13 G. A. Studdert-Kennedy, from "High and Lifted Up," in *The Sorrows of God and Other Poems* (Harper, 1924), p. 50.

   15–18 From "The Suffering God," in *Ibid.*, p. 12.

30 8–9   Heb. 11:1, R.S.V.

   17–20 John Greenleaf Whittier, "The Eternal Goodness," stanza 11.

   26–27 I John 5:4, R.S.V.

   32   II Cor. 12:7, R.S.V.

   36 ff. II Cor. 4:8–9, J. B. Phillips, *Letters to Young Churches* (Macmillan, 1957), p. 73.

31 35–36 William Williams, "Guide Me, O Thou Great Je-

Page Line

John Woolman (Macmillan, 1922), p. 161.

33–37   Quoted in Alexander Miller, *The Renewal of Man* (Doubleday, 1955), p. 100.

80   7–9   Thomas Carlyle, *Sartor Resartus,* Bk. II, Ch. 7 (Scribner, 1899), p. 131.

12–15   Victor Hugo, *Les Miserables.*

83   8 ff.   From a tribute given by the Hon. Charles E. Wyzanski, Jr., at a dinner by the Association of the Bar of the City of New York and the New York County Lawyers' Association, 1955.

15 ff.   From "Variations on an Undiscovered Theme," a poem written by Dr. MacLeish in honor of both Judge Augustus N. Hand and his son, the Hon. Learned Hand.

84   23–28   Arthur Miller, *Death of a Salesman* (Viking, 1949), p. 33.

86   18–24   William Shakespeare, *Hamlet,* Act 3, Sc. 2, lines 393–399.

87   8 ff.   John F. Kennedy, *Profiles in Courage* (Harper, 1956), p. 4.

92   18–19   William Shakespeare, *King Henry VIII*, Act 3, Sc. 2, line 441.

93   3–4   Rudyard Kipling, from *Barrack Room Ballads,* "The Ladies," viii.

95   31 ff.   Roland H. Bainton, *Pilgrim Parson* (Nelson, 1958), pp. 1, 2.

18–21   Kipling, "Glory of the Garden."

97   29–35   Edward Everett Hale, *For the Lend-a-Hand Society.*

100   1 ff.   Adolf Deissmann, *St. Paul, A Study in Social and Religious History* (Hodder and Stoughton, 1912), p. 66.

101   14 ff.   James M. Barrie, Rectorial Address at St. Andrews University, Scotland, May 3, 1922.

103   14–16   II Cor. 12:9, R.S.V.

108   7 ff.   William J. Lederer and Eugene Burdick, *The Ugly American* (Norton, 1958), p. 280.

110   6–7   In an address, "Science, Politics and Peace," to the New York Academy of Medicine, Jan. 7, 1960.

111   9 ff.   Gerald Clark in the *Montreal Star,* Dec. 10, 1958.

111   19–21   William R. Inge, *Diary of a Dean* (Hutchinson,

Page Line

1950), p. 154.

113   1–4   Quoted in J. Wallace Hamilton, *Ride the Wild Horses* (Revell, 1952), p. 44.

      19–20   Alfred Tennyson, from *Oenone*, "The Way to Power."

116   32–35   Edwin Markham.

118   26–32   Martin Luther King, Jr., *Stride toward Freedom* (Harper, 1958), p. 202.

119   3–5   C. Wright Mills, *The Causes of World War Three* (S. and S., 1958), p. 147.

120   27   H. G. Wells, in *Outline of History*.

122   18 ff. See Vance Packard, *The Hidden Persuaders* (McKay, 1957), p. 51.

127   5–6   Rom. 12:2, R.S.V.
      8   I Cor. 2:16.

129   26 ff. In the *New York Herald Tribune*, March 16, 1960.

130   33–34   Gen. 3:19, R.S.V.

134   21 ff. William Temple, *Citizen and Churchman* (Eyre and Spottiswoode, 1941), p. 100.

      27 ff. Leslie Weatherhead.

136   3–4   William Shakespeare, *The Merry Wives of Windsor*, Act II, Sc. 2, line 3.

138   1–7   Matt. 20:25–28, Author's translation.
      10–14   John 19:10, 11, R.S.V.

140   12–16   William James, *Letters*, Vol. II (Little, Brown, 1920), p. 90.

      31 ff. Arthur Daley, "Sports of the Times," in *The New York Times*, Oct. 15, 1951.

142   5–6   Matt. 16:24, R.S.V.

144   11 ff. Luke 14:8–10, Moffatt.
      24 ff. Mark 12:38–40, R.S.V.

145   17 ff. Mark 10:42; 9:35, R.S.V.

146   19 ff. As told in Henry Sloane Coffin, *Joy in Believing* (Scribner, 1956), p. 123.

      33–35   Matt. 5:13, 14; 5:48, R.S.V.

152   17 ff. As told in Halford E. Luccock, *Preaching Values in the Epistles of Paul* (Harper, 1959), p. 100.

158   29 ff. John 4:24; II Cor. 4:18, R.S.V.

159   25–28   Maltbie D. Babcock, "Give Us This Day Our Daily Bread."

Strengthening
The Spiritual Life

Nels F. S. Ferré

GUIDEPOSTS ASSOCIATES, INC.
Carmel, New York

STRENGTHENING THE SPIRITUAL LIFE

To My Sisters

Thyra Bjorn

Margaret Ferré

Ann Whitaker

Karin Herr

faithful co-workers in the

life of the Spirit

Contents

Contents

Preface

THE content of this book was delivered to the International Convention of Disciples of Christ. Through the courtesy of its executive secretary, Dr. Gaines M. Cook, these addresses are now offered to the general public.

I am deeply indebted to my wife and to Miss Marilynn Hindman for their constant co-operation during the writing of this book both in typing and in stylistic improvements. At this time, too, I want to acknowledge the warm feeling of gratitude I have toward all the members in the Religious Book Department of Harper & Brothers.

NELS F. S. FERRÉ

Nashville, Tennessee
September 11, 1950

Strengthening
the Spiritual Life

I

A Formula for Spiritual Success

"I have come to the seminary to learn to pray," said "Mother
Alice" Kahokuoluna of the Kalaupapa Leper Colony speaking in chapel. "That is my biggest need as I face my situation."
Deep in the pew I felt very small, knowing that we seminary
professors could teach other things far better than we could
teach that.

"Before the missionaries came to Hawaii," she went on in
effect, "my people used to sit outside their temples for a long
time meditating and preparing themselves before entering.
Then they would virtually creep to the altar to offer their petition and afterward would again sit a long time outside, this
time to 'breathe life' into their prayers. The Christians, when
they came, just got up, uttered a few sentences, said Amen
and were done. For that reason my people called them haolis,
'without breath,' or those who fail to breathe life into their
prayers."

Many of us feel today that the greatest challenge is to
breathe vitality into our spiritual life. Unless our life of the
spirit is strengthened we have no real hope. With it strengthened, we and our children can see an age fulfilling the hopes
we hardly dare cherish.

Our times need religion, not because nothing else is left, but
because there is nothing better. Social confusion, political insecurity, and military destruction beset us on every hand. The
church that was born to bless stands pretty much with empty
hands. It has lost heart. What voice it has gives utterance to
the ways of the world. The church speaks too often with the
wisdom of *Time* magazine and the realism of newspaper and
radio.

Most people are anxious. They worry. Little children, supposedly sheltered in Christian homes, have nightmares and wake up screaming that the Russians are coming. Even good Christian folk are doubting their faith. They wonder if its assurance is not garnish for a poisoned platter. They have come to suspect that the main dish is always bitter and fatal, religion with its trimmings being therefore a disguise of the true facts. Our age is sick of idealism and spews it out as a deceit.

Yet deep in their insides these same people have a lingering awareness of the realism of religion at its authentic best. They always did know that an easy religion is a false promise. True faith makes radical demands and commands radical treatments. Within their heart of hearts they are on the way to understanding that God's will for the common good is no sentimental idealism, but concrete living; that it alone can save us from our social confusion, our political insecurity, and our military annihilation.

Many times God speaks through dreams to those attentive to His voice. One night recently my wife dreamt that she was back in a college classroom with the assignment of an English theme on "How to Stop Worrying." As she sat gazing at the sheet of paper, wondering where to begin, she felt impelled to compose rapidly, in a hand not her own, a flow of inspired words. Upon awaking, she could remember only the three points of the outline: Worship, work, wait. I should like to prescribe this "divine formula" for all who need relief from worry, rest from work, and peace of heart for genuine well-being.

Worship is the baring of one's whole life unto God. Ritual is not worship. Worship is the finding and the acceptance of the real. Whatever the means used, worship is the soul's intercourse with God. Worship is not only the occasional standing on holy ground but the constant living on it. Worship comes from knowing what life is all about. Worship follows seeing and feeling beyond the fleeting moment. To worship is to be gripped by God. Worship—provided it is the worship of the true God—is the living in and by eternity. To worship aright is being invaded by the deathless freshness of eternal love and everlasting life. Such worship reveals life as it is and God as He is, and by the seeing of Him conquers every anxiety. This vision of God is a prescription for true peace and power and the cure for all worry.

Worship issues in adoration. One day after I had been weeks in pain to the point of utter discouragement, my Christian mother overheard me praying, "Dear Lord, if thou wilt ever have me well and use me again, thy will be done; if not, thy will be done anyway." "Nels," she reproved, "that's no way to pray. Thank Him and praise Him; thank Him and praise Him." This I did; then I better understood what adoration meant. God's will is constantly for the best, whatever happens. Come what may, He is to be thanked and praised.

Either we co-operate with Him or we do not. If we co-operate, He blesses us with His presence, whether we feel it or not. We get the chance to turn all suffering, loss, and limitation into the glorying in afflictions, the possession of nothing that makes us rich, the opportunity for healing faith and helping service. If this health and these open doors become ours, moreover, they become the means for good works and these, when others see them, cause them to praise our Father in heaven.

If, on the contrary, we fail to accept God's will for our good, our refusal finally thwarts us. He will not let us keep going forever our own foolish way. He makes the road ahead rough and threatening. Yet He is continually stretching out His arms to save us for His better way.

The sovereign Lord is saving love. To accept Him is to adore Him. To lack gratitude and joy is a failure to see and to accept the true and living God. Perfect love casts out fear. The worship of God is the end of worry. While we worship we cannot worry. But as long as we worry we cannot worship.

To worship God is to know that whatever happens is for the best. To be sure, our sin and foolishness are not good, but that we be both free and have a chance to learn is for the best. The depth of our trouble measures the strength of our freedom and the height of God's grace. Since God is sovereign love, all things work together for good to those who love Him. This good is the coming of His kingdom with power and speed. The more we love Him and the more we are who do love Him, the mightier and faster is the coming of His kingdom. When our hearts are in heaven we find our treasures in the doing and spreading of God's will among men.

This working together for good may seem anything but good to the unbeliever and the misunderstander. It may mean a cross, a crucifying of self and of all the self's works. But the worshiper glories in the cross where bane or blessing is sanctified. True, he never seeks the cross, but he is always willing to take it up and to bear it. The worshiper accepts both the cross and the crown with adoring acquiescence. While looking one night for a Scripture verse for meditation I happened to turn to a text promising that he who trusts God shall never be disappointed. My wife's comment was that most people would probably construe this to mean that everything would go well with them, humanly speaking! How much deeper lies the truth that he who lives in worship understands that God's ways are always best and that in accepting them he lives in adoration.

Worship also helps us see ourselves as we are and to see things as they are. What is stranger than ourselves? We know that hair turns gray, but how personal gray hair looks on ourselves! We know that people grow old and die, but how strange for *us* to have children in college or to have grandchildren. And how strange to face the inevitable end of this life. Perhaps stranger to some is to see themselves sinning, to feel themselves loved, to know themselves forgiven and in the presence of God. Most of the time, however, we are strangers to ourselves.

Nor can we even measure ourselves correctly. We hide from ourselves the parts which we do not like. We paint over such elements to make them seem strong and pretty; this we do with our eyes closed lest we should see ourselves as we are. We do not dare to face ourselves, for all our trying to change ourselves has failed. Only when we worship the living God do we dare accept ourselves as we are in the light and judgment of what we ought to be. For when we worship Him there is hope of forgiveness and promise of a new life. He sends forth judgment unto victory. Whatsoever is born of God overcomes the world.

To worship aright is not only to see ourselves but also to see things more clearly as they are. Public opinion is always being declared by neighbors, clubs, pulpit, press, movies, and radio. Commentators become professionally excited over every event. We feel lost in the tangle of propaganda emitted by interest groups. Only as we gain the perspective and proportion of God's work in history do we see what really is happening. Then we stand amazed at the unreality and false tensions of the world. Disasters bespeak God's constant judgment and prove His faithfulness. The deepest threats to our existence are the scales that weigh our aims. The victories of the world are scaled down to size. Small signs of the Spirit thunder their ultimate importance.

The pace of God, too, tests our own pace. His long-suffering purposes our salvation, and only as we know for certain in our hearts that love never fails and can never lose its own can we find the eternal relaxation which achieves the maximum through creative concern. Worship is the first and the preeminent prescription for worry. Worship is the finding of peace and power, for it is the living in the presence of God.

The second part of the formula on how to stop worrying was work. Only he who worships can labor to the fullest advantage, for all work is ordained by God for our true good. God gives us work to do because He shares with us His own creativeness. Jesus knew that his Father worked as well as he. The Sabbath symbolizes His day of rest, but the seventh day follows six days of work. The rest of God in fellowship, pure and full, is the climax of reality, but such rest follows and is dependent upon, to all eternity, six days of creative work. This ratio of work to rest is the proportion established by God's experience. We, too, as His children need the same proportion in our lives, if they are to find the purer and fuller rest of fellowship as a sabbath enjoyment.

Worry ceases when we work with God, for His work always counts. To work within His purpose for the common good is to find and to feel life's real meaning. Such work is the surest cure for the despair of futility. It gives zest to life because it helps human needs. No work is real unless it does. It also inspires us with the sense of victory, for God's work never fails. We know that we do God's work when we truly strive for the common good, not as pleasers of men but unto God.

Many work to "get ahead," which means to get themselves ahead. They find no escape from anxiety. They grow old swiftly, in spirit and in body, and even acquire headaches, nervousness, stomach ulcers and insomnia. He who cannot sleep because of a cup of coffee ought to examine his purpose in the struggle. Perhaps this turns out to be personal ambition —to receive glory from others and not the true glory of God. Others work to get money for pleasure, for display, or for security. They get no relief from anxiety. They know what worry means, but they fail to understand or to make use of the Bible's advice to take pleasure in their exertions.

Still others escape life in work. They think that while they are buried in work they are immune to worry. But they are not. Far from it. While their hands are busy their minds are busy too. Their temper grows short; their mood grows dark; their body shows the strain. No one can hide from God, no one can flee from others or even from himself, no matter how thick the barricade of work.

Work in itself, merely as activity, cannot satisfy the person's sense of meaning and of importance. When toil is solely a means and is not regarded as a medium of fellowship with God and men, people so engaged bend and twist their very natures and natural interests. But those who cannot enjoy the day or sleep at night soon lose the capacity to enjoy pleasure, esteem, or power. They are to be pitied who do not make a melody within their heart out of their work.

Those who work with a single heart unto God find joy and

strength and pleasure in their efforts. Even those who are not allowed to do what they crave can hear in the prison of circumstance a midnight song of deliverance. For working unto God always constitutes a light burden and an easy yoke. When work is worship God transfigures every task with His own presence, and the pay envelope occasions no protest. The New Testament can teach us this. Some speak of that book as reactionary, that it accepts the status quo, even slavery. How much deeper is its message. Personal attitudes in work and social relations will both be transformed, not through coercives of legislation nor even through social pressure, but mainly through an indwelling grace which transforms every circumstance and every relation, the master and the slave becoming brothers of each other in the Lord. Christianity does not mean the doing away with legitimately different economic functions. These are necessary to organized industry. But Christianity brings true democracy and the true sharing of the products of labor because of its spirit of common concern under God with whom there is no respect of person. A pity it is that most people consider this spiritual and social democracy as merely a beautiful theory. Nothing can more surely bring in the classless and raceless society as a real attitude than the Christian faith in actual practice.

Worship is man's most important work. To work is to direct one's efforts according to some purpose. We need play, too, purposeless effort for fun and relaxation. We need to have, even more, effortless fellowship. But real worship, correctly understood and pursued, is hard work. Through prayer, witness, and work we direct our lives to its central aim of loving God and making Him more loved by all people.

The preacher has no monopoly here. As long as the church witness is a solo rather than a chorus it is going to lack depth and volume. You cannot make the minister into a prima donna and expect a strong church. Only when all the members really unite at worshiping God with their whole life can the world become transformed by the power of the Gospel. Farmers, doctors, carpenters, lawyers, housewives, teachers, cattlemen

—all must practice to sing the new song of our common humanity unto the Lord of creative power. When worship becomes generally a steady job, and work our steady worship, the world shall see life assuming a new quality, a new you, a new peace, an absence of anxiety that shall make it take note and take heart. If we want to stop worrying we must make our work into worship and our worship into work so that the peak attainment of the six days of work may be reached in the pure fellowship of the seventh day of worship, and rest in God and with God.

The third article of the divine prescription against worry was wait. To wait is not easy. It is a hard lesson to learn. In patience we are promised to possess our souls, but how few of us succeed. Our capacity for waiting shows our concrete trust in God. God's way is not our way and God's pace is not ours. The less we are willing to wait the less we believe Him. Anxiety shows itself to a great extent in restlessness. People cannot even allow the muscles of their faces or their hands to relax. Worriers rub their hands, wash their hands, fiddle with their rings or watch chains, thump cigarettes, or dawdle with anything that is handy. They must ever be doing something. They do not like to be still even in church. Prolonged silence makes them nervous. Something must happen, and if they are not causing it, they are sure that nothing is happening.

On this subject I can speak from experience. As a child I was extremely high-strung. On school days I wanted to be wakened far too early and would run all the way to school as if the devil were after me. My father could not bear to wait for people. My mother dreaded keeping him waiting when he was going somewhere. Ever since childhood, too, I have had to fight a drive that rebelled against waiting. But God knew the cure. All my life I have had to wait abnormally long for many things which I wanted in a particular hurry. The fever of life made me fret and fume on such occasions; and often I must have been hard on those who had to wait with me. Such real victory as I have experienced—and it is genuine and by no means petty—has come through prayer and total surrender to God's will. Most of the hurry was self-will and not concern for others; it was a trusting of myself rather than of God.

Some people cannot trust themselves enough to believe that what is done well and with a good intention can be let go. They are always berating themselves for what they did or did not do and stewing over the results. They cannot wait to grow themselves and to see their work ripen. Nor can they wait to be corrected by time. They must be perfect and above blame right away. They therefore picture themselves and their work in a false light and sputter when they are not recognized or their deeds are not appreciated.

Nor can they trust others. They cannot delegate responsibility. Unless they do the thing themselves they feel that nothing will be done right; at least they cannot wait and see. Nor can they wait to let others grow. They do things for their children to get them done properly. Then they worry because they have not time for everything, because they get no rest, because their children do not mature and assume responsibility, because everyone considers them bossy and prefers for fellowship others who do not "amount to" so much as they. The world can do little with these self-serious perfectionists. They cannot know fellowship, for they trust only themselves. Other people are unreal and they cannot take time for them to show what they can do, what responsibility they can shoulder, or what capacity for growth is in them.

Harder still is it to wait for God. His patience seems slackness. After all, He has eternity and our concern is present time. The world is wrong and we are here to right it, and at once. The zeal of many a reformer is disguised atheism. Much desire to please others is nervous self-protection. What God wants, however, is relaxed, trustful waiting.

Obviously not all waiting is good. Some escape life into spiritlessness. They have no energy because they dare not face life. They are tired and suffer from low blood pressure because of worry. Both high and low blood pressure, both stomach ulcers and lack of appetite may be signs of worry and of a lingering death. Some people dread making decisions and put off action as long as possible. Some have their security in things as they are and would wait forever before attempting anything new. Waiting may be the result of laziness or indifference. Certainly we must not exalt waiting into the essence of faith.

Nevertheless experience does work patience, when experience is itself worked over in worship. Real waiting is concerned waiting. It is more than interested watching. It is feeling and knowing oneself involved in the outcome. It is being personally invested in the result. It is love's being with and for those who must do the deciding for themselves. Real waiting is also expectant waiting. Love never fails. Christian concern hopes all things. It is continually on the edge of seeing things happen. Christian waiting finds things done according to its faith. It may find open results and rejoice. It may find the patience of unanswered prayer and rejoice. It is never wearied in well-doing when that well-doing is misinterpreted or rejected. Christian waiting witnesses in season and out of season. Fainting not, it reaps in due time. When that time is due God knows, and His blessing is always on time.

Real waiting is also victorious waiting. We have unsolvable problems, but God has none. We have permanent problem children, but He does not. We die and do not see the fruits of our labor in this life, but God never dies and beyond this life we shall see the reward of every deed done in the body. Real waiting is victorious waiting because though our warfare seems constant the outcome is certain.

Those who are on God's side never know final defeat. They cannot feel sorry for themselves because they are edged out of positions of influence, because they are kept from leadership, because even their motives are stigmatized. They bear on their body only the stigmas of their Lord and they witness to the power of the sons of the resurrection. Real waiting is living within the quiet joy and peace of God's own way, more natural than the return of the salmon to its breeding place or of the waterfowl to its summer nest. Such waiting is the cure for worry, for it is living within the perspective, pace, and proportion of God. Such waiting is peace and power.

Real waiting is the soul's sabbath rest amidst the unrest and confusion of the workaday world.

This, then, is the divine prescription against worry; this is the divine cure of anxiety; this is the divine healing for spirit, mind, and body: Worship, work, wait. We turn now to consider more concretely ways of personal, family, and group devotions, with the confidence that anyone who faithfully follows this prescription cannot only stop worrying but also find, surprisingly, peace of mind, peace of soul, and the peace of God which passes all understanding.

II

Strengthening Through Personal Devotions

PRAYER is man's most accessible means to the greatest possible power. Not only can we bring about a whole new world through prayer but one's own life can by its means become astonishingly new. The sick, the crippled, the shut-in, and the imprisoned can pray with the same power as can the strong man and the influential woman. The child is heard by God as are the aged and the dying. Although prayer is everywhere available it is nevertheless almost universally wasted and neglected. What can be more important, therefore, than that each one of us learn to use better this great gift of God?

We are not going to argue about the reality and power of prayer. The giants of religion have been men of prayer; they were not great for themselves but for the world, thereby changing the world, as well as themselves, for the better. "The saints who changed the world" is no mere phrase; they were history's most real people. Instead of arguing about them we must take up their task. This we cannot do, however, apart from prayer. No one can improve the world drastically and with such speed as is now needed except God; and He, respecting our freedom, will not do so apart from our co-operation. Our fullest co-operation can come only through the community of prayer. We all need to learn to pray better; this is life's most important lesson.

Only by praying can this lesson be learned. There is no way to acquiring skill except by doing. Theoretically a man may study to throw ringers in horseshoes; actually to throw them he must practice for the peg. Many truths about prayer can be explored through theory but no learning will become personal experience and reality apart from the doing. Every skill takes time and patience, but the reality of prayer, being life's chief lesson, is therefore also its hardest. Prayer as communion with God, the center of life, can never be mastered easily. The very difficulty shows its importance and reality. Yet it is a lesson which all must learn sooner or later, in this life or beyond, for the career of one's soul itself is measured by it. Every other attainment is ultimately for the sake of this one, making prayer for the wise person the primary aim of his life. Our knowing and loving God, our concern for the world, our personal fulfillment and satisfaction—all are drawn together in the reality and progress of our prayer life. Prayer, then, is first on life's agenda and no one can afford to be unconcerned about it.

Now, I want to share with you a few hints from my personal experience as to how the practice of prayer may be improved. The first rule we all need to learn is relaxation. We cannot come into the divine presence tense and terse and expect to meet the divine. In this state of tension we are still very much involved in ourselves. We have to let go. Such letting go is true of life as a whole. A report has it that a large sum was spent in teaching Ted Williams to relax at the batter's plate. A golfer will shoot fairly well until he is obsessed to do better. Then he usually becomes tense and does far worse! God has made the world self-defeating for the self-serious! Relaxation is needed in prayer as in everything else.

How can this be accomplished? Each person, naturally, must find his own best way. There is no substitute for personal experience. It is better, nevertheless, to lie in bed while praying in order to relax than to kneel in stiff discomfort on a stone floor. There are moods, to be sure, when falling on one's knees or stretching out one's arms while standing are entirely appropriate. My own deepest experience, for instance, came while kneeling in my customary prayer corner. But for long sustained prayer the body should be at ease. Jesus may have prayed sitting on a ledge or a hillside through early morning hours. Comfortable sitting or lying I believe to be important aids to relaxed prayer. The many years I had to pray while sick in bed taught me this lesson.

There are also concrete aids to relaxation. One such aid is literally to take one's whole self and place it in God's hands, saying: "Holy Spirit, take me as I am and do thou help me to pray. Here I put myself in thy hands completely. Receive me completely, both my willing and my unwilling parts." In my own case I feel physical surrender starting to overspread me from above my eyebrows. Conscious relaxation of wrists, ankles, and neck also help in the physical preparation.

For a reason unknown to me I have also found that a surrendered, steady upward turning of my closed eyes has not only unbound me, but released in me some creative flow that causes the whole body to flush with a sense of well-being. Something of the same effect is had when, in imagination, I let my whole self sink back as though my head were being lowered on an uptilted cot. These techniques are physically effective to the point that I have long hesitated to use or to mention them, for in theory, wanting pure spirituality, I have been afraid of any bodily approach, and certainly of every technique. I have wondered where this creative surge would take me. The more I have prayed, however, the more I have discovered how God uses such means; the actual result has been health and creative zest, a happy family, and many more open doors in my work. I have therefore decided to give God the glory by the sharing of these experiences for what they may be worth to other seekers. In any case, bodily relaxation I believe to be of utmost importance for effective prayer.

Along with relaxation comes recollection. The order here is not fixed. Genuineness and naturalness are most important. Discipline is good and some order is necessary to steady growth, but order can become a rut and discipline a mere habit. Sometimes we wake up practically with a shout of glory, knowing ourselves to be in God's presence and suffused with adoration and joy. The more fully prayer possesses the heart, the longer, the more natural is such experience of immediate adoration. But for most beginners there is prior need of willed relaxation and recollection.

Recollection involves first of all the recalling of who God is.

God is sovereign love. He is both ultimate reality and our most intimate friend. We should not pray as pagans, bowing and scraping or pleading to be heard. God is more real and near than we are and wants to have fellowship with us far more than we want it with Him. *To be able to remember who God is, is perhaps the hardest prerequisite of true prayer.* We tend to treat God as though He were one of us. We endow Him with our own love of glory, desire for revenge, or hardness of heart. Either that or He is not real to us and we try to make Him real by dint of much fervor and hard praying. We keep forgetting that if we will but call on Him honestly, He hears and helps us more than we can ask or think.

The second thing to recollect is that God loves everyone completely. Somehow or other it is hard not to think of oneself as a favorite child. We want to get something from God for ourselves alone. Much of such praying hurts us and we should be better off not praying at all. By praying in that way we get even more wrapped up in ourselves and farther away from God. Instead we should always recall that God is always completely for all, and that we cannot pray to Him aright unless we are completely surrendered to the common good. Our answered prayer may, in fact, be a cross borne for the common welfare. Or our best blessing may be given to us precisely in order for us to give it to others.

Only within this view of God ought we to remember how He also cares completely for us and how we can take to Him our every care and problem. Sometimes we try to play God by practicing love to all without recognizing how deeply we most of all need God Himself and His care if we are to be enabled to bless others and humble enough to be blessed by them.

Conscious relaxation keeps us from rushing thoughtlessly into the holy presence. Recollection makes us recall with whom we have dealing. God is completely ready to forgive and He never holds a thing against us, as might an offended human being. He grieves rather over the fact that we will not trust His love enough to forsake those ways which keep us from Him. Knowing that He longs to forgive and to restore us in order that we might walk in the newness of life, we must therefore lift up our lives to be restored by His faithfulness.

We do not realize our own deepest need for restoration. Because sin has clouded our vision we see ourselves mostly as good. Therefore we defend ourselves from the hurt of failure and from the sting of guilt. But prayer restores the Publican who knows he is a sinner, and leaves Pharisee unchanged who is conscious of his good deeds. If we feel no need for restoration we are very likely self-righteous. When our guilt becomes unbearable we may develop into a self-righteousness which is a form of mental illness. Some fanatical leaders, for instance, are very prone to think that they are God's anointed while they are closer to being candidates for the asylum. Forms of the Christian faith which stress sinlessness are particularly tempted in this respect. All of us, however, need to pray for forgiveness and the restoring of the joy of our salvation.

Prayer is communion. At times it consists in talking with God. But much communion ought to be spent in silence. Happy lovers know the depth of wordless fellowship. Constant jabbering wearies. The more we know and love God the more we ought to practice wordless prayers. In the deepest moments of their lives men are struck dumb and numb not only with sorrow but with deep joy. Since prayer is fellowship we ought to insure quietness in order to listen. How otherwise are we to hear? God does not speak with certainty to those who cannot hear the still small voice.

Yet, deeper than the silence of listening is the silence of communion. Mystics have called this union, rather than communion. But the merger of spirits is no merger of personalities. Beyond the abstractive powers of consciousness and the strains of personal individuality, oneness in holy communion is a high and holy reality. Though I am here putting silence early in the period of prayer, profound silence, where the soul is bathed in the love of God through wordless surrender and communion, should occur intermittently throughout any prolonged experience of it.

Generally prayer is supposed to begin with adoration. For full-fledged saints this is very likely the practice. Sometimes many also wake with such joy or go apart to pray with such exultation that nothing but the pure adoration of God seems to matter. Other times we need preparation of spirit before we can genuinely adore God. When we really know who God is and trust that all is eventually for the best, we cannot help adoring Him. Adoration cannot be forced. Adoration is the self's finding reality and rest. Adoration is the vision of God and feeling the fruition of His love. Adoration is the soul's sabbath experience, as whoever has tasted it knows. Anyone who was ever raised to the seventh heaven in or out of the body understands this "fragment of the future."

Gratitude follows adoration as night the day. We praise God for Himself, for His love and even our own blessings are acknowledged in humble thanksgiving. Life is new and rich and hopes abound unto thanksgiving. Within this exultant gratitude the longing steals to bless others and to serve. Thus intercession and petition for service begin to pour out along with the thanksgiving. No neat boundaries can be drawn for the rich prayer life. Adoration, thanksgiving, love, the desire to bless, the urge to be better, the will to please God and to help others, all interweave, then stream off into separate strands only to flow together in some other channel.

When we pray, however, we have the right to examine the spirit. We may often speak with spontaneous tongues, but in general there ought to be decency and order even in personal prayer life. The content of our prayer life ought to revolve around two focal points: We need to pray both from God's perspective and from our own. The Lord's Prayer is a perfect illustration of this truth. If we really adore and love God, we must try to see everything from His point of view. When doing so, we rejoice in God's eternity, in His eternal creations beyond our knowing, in His sure saving of all men in His time and way. Then we live in glory with the saints who have prepared the way. Jesus, "the forerunner," becomes the pioneer of our own faith.

Then all religions can be surveyed as man's seeking after God and God's letting himself be known at divers times and places. All questings become strangely dear, while in the same insight an urge to show the full love of God in Christ becomes our constant concern. Somehow, when God's perspective is accepted we behold our true transiency within the vast processes of God's eternity; but we see also the endless meaning of our lives within the purposes of God. We may find an aid in steadfastly imagining God's eyes looking down, down with love to all men, waiting for us to do our part. And His hand rests on our shoulder as we keep repeating "Lord here am I; use me."

We need also to pray from our own point of view, not selfishly, of course, but from the station where God has put us and from which He can use us and us alone. This place is our locus of responsibility and our chance to bless. Thus we offer up our own lives to God's service, come what may. We ask Him to do anything He pleases with us, to deliver us from all self-concern, to free us from prejudice and smallness of heart, to mingle our lives with the hosts of God who work trustfully for the coming of His Kingdom. We may then lift up our families, member by member, examining our own failures in relation to them, asking for concrete concern and actual thoughtfulness, and beyond that for our Father's richest blessing on their lives. We cannot pray for their external welfare and success, but that God's full will be done in each one of them, that He may be real to them, and that life's best blessings may come to them in whatever form God wants to give it. We may after that enter into our own gift of ancestry, thanking God for our forebears, generations back, and asking that we be worthy of their legacy, even increasing their faithfulness.

Then we may naturally branch out into the needs of relatives beyond the immediate family, close friends, and particularly into the necessities of those who are on our special list. Over the years we meet those who ask for our prayers or who become our particular charges. We may go on to bless our local church, the various churches, the Church Universal and its leaders. We may pray for different branches of faith. Or we may intercede for institutions which train the clergy, particularly the teachers of the ministry.

We may pray, also, for missionaries, now in one country then in another, or for people we know all over the world. Or we may pray for community leaders, teachers, labor leaders, leaders of business or professions, housewives, college students, patients in hospitals, convicts in prison, for our country, for so-called enemy countries, for the United Nations. There seems to be no end to the objects of our petitions, and the more we pray the more we have to keep selecting items for special stress. Somehow, too, all of life comes closer and we sense our belonging to all God's creatures as we pray for them and love them with God's concern. Very likely we end our prayer with thanksgiving and by committing all things into God's care and keeping. Best of all is the closing of prayer with silent communion.

Amid the hustle and bustle, however, where there never is time enough for what we have to do, how can there possibly be time for such praying? Preachers may find it, but can a layman? During years of sickness when I could not sleep for pain, I discovered the joy and strength of praying at night. Like the monks who used to get up various times during the night to worship God, I would lie back letting myself sink into God. Too weary to struggle, throwing my spent self on the Holy Spirit, I experienced real rest and an unmistakable inflow of power. My body began to flush with new life. Much sleeping is "for sorrow." It is due to tension and is an escape from trouble. When all is surrendered, the spirit, body, and mind find such rest in prayer that instead of having less energy a new creative force emerges. Of late years I have discovered the possibilities of early morning. Jesus himself knew this secret and used it. Even a married man whose early rising would wake his wife and children can nevertheless lie reverently in bed and pray through the early morning hours. A specific time need not be set, for God wakes His own lovers early enough for the purpose.

Another valuable prayer time is just before work. Prayer starts the work right. But everybody must find his own time and method. A farmer can pray on the tractor; a housewife, while doing dishes, or while ironing. Instead of listening to the radio or reading the newspaper one can listen to God and meditate on high matters. Prayer brings relaxation and rest after a hard day. A girl in love always finds time to think of her lover regardless of how busy she is. Anyone who loves God finds ample time to share God's concern each day. A particularly good opportunity for praying is afforded by traveling on trains or on buses, or while driving a car.

Prayer should provide the constant set of the self. As soon as the spirit is freed from concentration on work or on company, one rises to God in praise and holy communion. When we think of friends or meet people, the heart jumps up to bless them without them knowing it. When we enter a new city we bless it. When we read a new book we bless its writer and its reading. When we hear a speaker we cannot help exalting him to be used by God, and we pray that our own lives may be readied for the fullest response.

Made inwardly rich through constant prayer, we may begin to hear almost constant voices. How shall we treat these voices? First, let us be thankful for them. Prayer is conversation and the spirit speaks in quiet and real communion with those who cultivate such prayer. Secondly, we shall test them by the simple method of lifting them up to the Holy Spirit, saying in effect, "I can't know for certain if this be thy voice; O Lord, do thou show me more plainly. Particularly deliver me from subtly suggesting my own will." If the voice persists and is in line with God's concern for the common good, we can accept it and act upon it. God can use autosuggestion, if acceptance be that. If the voices prove sometimes mistaken, that should not make an end to praying. Trust God and go on to victory.

After years of hearing such voices a pattern of answer will become compellingly real, including perhaps astonishing predictions or actual healings. One should avoid talk about these voices, however, and not depend upon them as final authorities. Rejoice, rather, that God is faithful. Fellowship is far more important than power to know or to do. By all means refrain from making the rule that the voice must go against the inclinations. Such promptings may be due to fear or to the will to die. *Rather, test the voices thankfully and believingly according to God's concern for the common good.* Let every blessing bless and let God abound to you and through you.

Again, to depend upon feelings is dangerous. You may learn after a while that when you feel weakest God is doing the most through you. Did not even Jesus feel that he could do nothing in himself? When God seems almost absent to you, someone else may find God compellingly real through your life. The closer you live to God, however, the more should hope abound and joy flood your soul. You should learn to rejoice always. If such joy is not a common occurrence you are not praying right. Our faith is a Gospel. Perhaps you need to learn the lesson of simplicity, to trust God as a small child trusts his father. The Christian also stops pretending. He becomes open and simple. Sophistication is the wisdom of the wise, and this is foolishness to God. By simple trust in God's absolute love your feelings become genuinely positive; and the more you trust, the more you will find both the inner peace and the outer poise you seek.

Finally, give God glory without show. Avoid unnatural piety. Jesus told us to anoint our faces so that people will not see that we fast, and to pray in the inner closet. Nevertheless, your light is not to be hid under a bushel or a bed. Live openly, though humbly, the power of the Gospel. Let your life testify to God's grace. If He has healed you, proclaim thankfully His praise. If He has prospered you, never claim for yourself the power to cause growth or to give increase. If He has put you in the shadow, dwell there in order to bear witness to the power of light to overcome it. If you face failure and death, testify through both to God's total victory.

God is concerned to use your life. May your prayer life be so relaxed and so filled with recollection, that you may feel the joy of your salvation restored through forgiveness, and in silent adoration thank Him. Thus by lifting up His Kingdom and all your own concerns under Him, you may steadily hear His voice of warning or of approval and may feel Him so real and near that others will testify to the Gospel of the grace of God declared in your life. Each one of us can improve his own prayer life; the exact way must be discovered by every individual until he knows the Spirit's manner of working. But for each one of us there is waiting an ever fuller satisfaction and usefulness of life through prayer.

III

Strengthening Through Family Devotions

WIN the family for Christian living and the world is won. The family is the seat of our basic troubles and the source of our noblest hopes. This claim is no mere theory. This is factual truth.

We now know how deeply children are affected by their homes. For a while some psychologists went to extremes, teaching that children are permanently formed in infancy. This is not true. Human nature is plastic and continually open to change. It is most plastic, however, in early childhood; and character is more basically set there than some like to think. Our parents do not stop disciplining us when the physical action of spanking stops nor do they cease spoiling us when we leave home. Their dispositions, right or wrong, become formative conditions of our lives with which we have to contend as long as we live.

The fruit seldom falls far from the tree. Sometimes it is carried elsewhere by extraneous forces. Not only apples but children are picked up and planted, for good or for ill, in alien soil. No parent should therefore judge himself completely responsible for the conduct of a wayward child nor must he boast too personally of a successful offspring. There is real freedom for the child, and other influences than parental ones help make him what he is. But for the most part the fruit falls near by. Children are usually mirrors in whom parents can see reflected their own images. For this reason, because of their own guilt, the older generation tends to be either too hard or too easy on its successor.

Jesus grasped the right formula for a new life. "Make the

tree good." The good life can bear good fruit, not only in thoughts and deeds, but especially in good children. The most important crop to care for is the family fruit. The surest way to strengthen the spiritual life is to strengthen the spiritual life of the family. Children, to become creative and co-operative members of the family, need to experience genuine love at home from their early infancy. Newer understanding of physical beginnings makes the serene, believing mother a blessing even before the child is born. She who carries a new life may care for her child's basic spiritual structure more than she thinks by leading a life holy unto the Lord and peaceful for the world.

Children need a constant home environment of genuine love. Pious phrases or forced grins cannot fool them. They know love with their whole being and can separate appearance from reality. When parents abide in God's love day by day both with each other and with the children, that love becomes the source of the child's most basic security. Sham makes children detest the creed the parents profess. Rebellious ministers' children seek the reality of love away from all its false pretenses. Marriage quarrels are bad and sharp words hurt the children, but what really counts is the steady reality of the parents' love for each other and for them.

"Blow-outs" can be forgiven and erased, and do not act as hindrances to renewed community experience on a high level, but lack of love kicks the emotional underpinning from under the child. For the children's sake—and they constitute the coming world—the parents must therefore find love. The test of such love is whether each carries the concerns of the other in his heart, whether he wants to shield his partner from blame or to blame her when something untoward has happened, whether he subordinates his personal desires to the family welfare, and grows to have no desire save the family happiness, or whether he wants what he wants when he wants it, whether he disciplines and eradicates personal faults or rationalizes them into virtues.

Husbands, too, are often made or broken by their family

life. Behind successful men often stand women who are themselves emotional successes. They may be of different types. Some may constitute the serene background of emotional stability, symbolizing and enacting spiritual strength. Others may be secure leaders from whom the husbands gather both inspiration and actual guidance. Still others may be constant co-operators in a common venture. In all cases, however, they provide the home life which the husband needs and give him a chance to contribute his best.

To be sure, unmarried men and unhappily married men have often become famous, but the contribution of the well-rounded, naturally-balanced man has within it an unequaled fullness and effectiveness. For the steady welfare of society the world depends upon happily married people.

This is equally true of women. The loving husband, in fact, will want his wife to find life's greatest happiness, whether by letting her have the children she craves, devote herself to family work devoid of straining decisions, co-operate with him in his work, or even find expression in achievements of her own.

Not only for individuals, however, whether children, husbands, or wives, but also for the church the family is the primary unit. Adults can be won more easily for the church through concern for their children than through any other motive. Here is the opportunity of the church, often mentioned but seldom used. Let families be shown concretely spiritual living, therefore, and let the church be concerned with families as such.

The corporate nature of the church and of the family in the church should be maintained as well as discussed. Yet how few families constitute a church at home, and how few worship as families in public. If this cannot be done without disturbing the minister and congregation, something is radically wrong and the worship is faulty. Let reverence and discipline plus hallowed joy incorporate the small family community within the larger local church until both unite intensively and extensively in expressing and fostering the family of God. When that happens within the very fiber of family life the best human material for a better world has united with the fullest divine means. Win the family for the Christian enterprise, then the world is saved.

The family will not be won, however, without an effective approach through the devotional life. We tend to ignore this center of Christian living, as if it would take care of itself. Evil wins by default. We blame our busy schedules. Father must hurry to work. Or mother has to get the children to school. Or brother has his vacation and is entitled to sleep in the morning or to be with his date at night. There is thus no time for family devotions. Others dismiss it as old-fashioned. It is as passé, they feel, as the three-hour sermon.

But family devotions are the most important part of family life. The family altar stands unavoidably at the center of its life, lit and used, or dark and abused. The family is a church by nature, a community under God, either free and outreaching or frustrated and self-concerned. There is always time for what is deemed important. The fault lies not in our lack of time but in our sense of values. What is time for, and how is it to be used by a Christian family if no time is allowed for worship?

The proper time can be found somehow. Families can get up half an hour earlier. Much sleep is wasted by tensions. The worshiping family finds rest and peace in its worship. A new happiness can heal and refresh the weary spirit. So wake the sleepy boy! Shake the drowsy girl! Leave the dishes on the table and the newspaper on the front step and join in duty or in joy the feast of family devotions! Some can do it at night, if the ages of the children permit. Or time can be taken before breakfast or dinner. Special services may be held on Sundays, holidays, or days of celebration. The time is there! Members away from home can read the same passages and pray together in memory, in the divine presence and in anticipation of reunion. Sometimes people may have to have devotions in smaller family sections, through force of circumstance. The Christian family, in any case, lives by family devotions.

Strengthen those and you strengthen the family. Win the families and you win the world.

But how is family devotion conducted? If anyone can sing, and if one member can play an instrument, Christian hymns can be sung as a family. We begin our own family devotion each day that way. If each member chooses the hymn of the week, how many hymns soon become the rich background of later life. What a priceless Christian heritage to acquire! Let the baby choose "Jesus Loves Me" and do not tire of the simple words. Sing the adolescent hymns of youth, sharing your young girls' fervor, and live with the sophisticated taste of your college boy. Let the whole family breathe in the beauty of Bach. All must unite in any individual's selection of personal hymns, and no one need suppress his taste for Gospel songs or for hymns of the social gospel as well as for the great affirmations of faith in word and melody. Vigilance is necessary lest such hymn singing degenerates into routine. If the words are not being memorized, they are not being thought while sung.

Use song also as a means of fellowship. How near to your wife you are when you hear her play and sing or when you spend an occasional hour that way. How your boy will be one with you while you sing hymns together. Let the children play their instruments, well or haltingly, and sing with them. Learn to sing as a family in the car. Play alphabet games with Christian songs and make melody with united hearts. Choose theme songs for trips so that all may join reverently in joyful praise or prayer. Or gather around the radio and sing with the programs. Or sit around the fire and sing to the Lord. Stand together in church and hear the young ones let out their voices on the hymns they have learned at home. If at all possible strengthen the spiritual life of the family through song. If the history of a hymn can be obtained, that hymn becomes more meaningful. Some member of the family could make such information a hobby.

Family reading is also of great importance. The Bible should be read each day. We read it in successive portions only when all members living at home are present. It does not take long to get through the New Testament by reading only one paragraph each day in the Revised Standard Version. Sometimes the father will read aloud and all those who can read will follow along in their own Bibles. Sometimes another member will take over. Or sometimes verses may be read in turn. Selected passages from the Old Testament are also suitable for family reading. Much Old Testament material, however, is better covered through readings in the Children's Bible or in books of Old Testament stories, and not as family devotions.

Discussion of what is read should be natural. If discussion is not spontaneous, that shows either too much hurry or not enough interest. Significant comments can be elicited from children. It is advisable to read both King James, for its majestic beauty, and modern translations. If various members have different versions they often pipe up with great excitement when differences of meaning are discovered. Such differences tend to teach youngsters not to take the Bible at too literal a level. One or more commentaries should be handy. Actually the use of commentaries need consume very little time. What can better overcome Biblical illiteracy than such an introduction to the Bible at home as a part of family life?

The family should not, of course, stop with the Bible nor with formal devotional reading. There is good material available in books about the Bible or in selected stories from it. Numerous devotional manuals of real help are available like the *Upper Room*. Our family has profitably read and discussed for years *The Fellowship of Prayer*. Some of the best Advent booklets, like Dwight Bradley's *The Secret Stair*, for example, have enriched our Christmas seasons. Our children found Jones' *The Way to Power and Poise* a bit heavy but profited much by it. It is hard to convey how much joy and instruction we have received from *Pilgrim's Progress, The Eagle Series,* booklets on the lives of missionaries that fascinate the youngsters, and similar standard treasures. There is some biographical and fictional material suitable for family use, but we need much more. No family must ever be so busy or so indifferent that they fail to find the rich rewards awaiting them in this sphere of Christian literature.

Family prayers should be simple and natural. We find kneeling to be generally the best position to assume. When the floor is drafty, however, or when some member of the family does not get dressed on time, common sense must govern the matter of posture. The children catch their parents' attitudes. If they truly pray in the Spirit the children know it. If they do it mostly as a duty the children soon sense that. Then, if ever, the parents need to relax, to recall to whom they are praying and to feel the divine restoration, in order for the family altar to become the joy and power it ought to be.

In our circle we begin by letting the youngest pray first. Children can pray before they can talk. The baby will learn by feeling the emotional warmth of a mother's or father's prayers. He may slip in and out between the parents' knees, but as soon as he begins to talk at all he will join in the amens. It is surprising how soon an infant will participate in the Lord's Prayer with which we end our daily devotions. As soon as he can speak the baby can be taught to pray for the dear ones and to say "Thank you, Father." From then on the child will pray more maturely as he grows, and as he learns from his parents and older brothers and sisters. Very often a child's prayer will be dull and scattered. But that is no shortcoming. That is the way of life. And frequently children will startle their elders by the depths of their insights and by the sterling qualities of their sympathies.

After the youngest child has finished we pray in turn according to age, ending with the father of the family. We do so even when visitors are present. Christians are never embarrassed by their ages. Occasionally one or the other parent may have to recall for the family how important the meeting with God really is and help lift the prayer to a higher level. Most important, is the genuineness of the experience of God and the lifting up of the occasion for the Spirit to take charge beyond our faltering speech and wavering attention.

Family prayers, however, are of little worth unless the family has a real sense of family vocation. When the whole family shares day by day in what the breadwinner is doing, not only in conversation about it but in dedication before God, somehow the truth that man cannot live by bread alone becomes vitally apparent. As each child raises to God his parents and their work, a common sense of challenge and of achievement grips the family. In our own family the children put upon me an ever deeper obligation as they keep praying that God may give me the right words to say or to write. When I am away from home, I am never without the assurance of being lifted up in prayer by the family I have left behind. When I face a trying occasion the face of my wife at prayer flashes on my mind, banishing doubt and instilling joy and confidence. God uses the whole family. He promises that the prayers of even two or three for the coming of the Kingdom will be heard. How much, then, can a believing family achieve? Individualsim is destroyed, individuals become merged, and social motivation becomes real. We have had children visit us who have prayed with such beauty for their parents' work, that we have actually witnessed how every honest vocation can be felt, enjoyed, and enacted together by a truly praying family.

The basic vocation of the family is not the father's or mother's personal profession. Each family is an intensive unit whose most important job is to be the church, the family of God on a small scale. Each family has as its primary and main task to glorify God and to hasten the coming of His Kingdom. In this calling what each member does, from the oldest to the youngest, is thus of complete importance. Every member of the family must be aware of what each of the others is doing and enter into it with total abandon. Each member lifts up all the others in prayer, remembering their needs, cares, or particular doings for the day. Whenever something significant, good or ill, happens to any member all the others are ready to bear and to share it.

By means of such prayer one's sense of values is altered. Parents do not want their children to shine in school or in the club in order to gratify them. Neither do they want the children to work off their own frustrations. Rather they would have their children be Christian and do their best as Christians above all else. Parents pray that their children may hallow God's name and strive to serve humanity. A narrow competitive spirit is thus broken through and the co-operative attitude takes its place. The family is not pitted against other individuals or families. The parents are concerned that the children be thoughtful of other children's feelings; that they do not make them feel inferior. They want their children to be genuine. The children also know that they are loved for themselves, for what they are, and not because they win prizes and reflect credit on their parents.

Where else can the children learn so well the meaning of the social or co-operative spirit? If the children truly feel that the parents want above all to be good neighbors, that they really want to help and to honor those whom they deal with, the children have already caught such attitudes. Our world is perishing for lack of social motivation. We say that the world could be different if it were not for human nature. We could treat the races differently if only we could eradicate the prejudices which exist. We could have a different economic order if only we could cultivate individual initiative and responsible concern in such a manner that the use of property for the common good would not mean totalitarianism and bureaucracy. We could overcome nationalism if only early juvenile emotions would not block adult perception. We could do away with denominationalism if we could only attain a vision of the common good which yet permits differences of expression. Where, however, can such feelings be learned as well as in the Christian family?

We need a sense of vocation in our work. This is a large undertaking, and the major part of it must be accomplished at home. Let the family find the meaning of its common task around the family altar. What lies outside and beyond consists in letting the domestic hearth reflect and make real God's family of all mankind. When the wholeness of the human race becomes real through the single family and when the real vocation of the latter envisages all society as a community of common concern under a common God, then alone can the family achieve its end and life take on its deepest meaning.

The Christian family can best break down social barriers and cement satisfactory community relations. It can widen the horizons of understanding and co-operation unto the bounds of the world and until the end of time. Win the family effectively for Christ and you will win the church and the world. Strengthen the spiritual life of the family, in all aspects and dimensions, and you will hasten in the surest way the coming of the Kingdom of God.

IV

Strengthening the Spiritual Life

WE HAVE now considered the divine formula for spiritual success and for personal and family devotions. The spiritual life does not come easily. It is worth too much for that. It must be worked at, long and hard. In the present chapter we are to consider some further aspects of the kind of living that bears rich spiritual fruit when pursued with complete seriousness.

We must consider more fully the matter of reading. Far too little reading is done to feed the spiritual life, and often this reading is done in the wrong way. Naturally, our first concern is with the reading of the Bible. When the Bible is read in the light of the largest logic of God's love, the soul begins to feel its small walls shake and fall. Unless the Bible provides ever receding horizons it is being improperly read. The only right way to read the Bible is to learn how great and good God is, to feel one's narrowness judged and one's lack of faith, and to accept day by day larger loyalties and aims.

The most important suggestion perhaps is that the Bible be read slowly. Very likely much more is learned from the Bible when two or three verses are pondered each day than when a chapter is skimmed quickly. Pray as the Bible is opened that the heart and mind be prepared to receive and to appropriate. Approach the Bible devotionally. Such an approach does not involve a superstitious awe but a reverent respect. It does not presuppose authority, artificially imposed, that God's truth does not admit our questions. Instead the devotional attitude involves a recognition of the God who speaks in the Bible, of the central importance that the Bible has had for the saints as the standard of their faith, and of all that one's own experience has taught in living with it. The mind should be brought along, however, and not parked outside. One should be as thoughtful as possible of what is read in the Bible, for only thus can one discriminate between its local application and its spiritual meaning for us.

Certainly if the Christ had to come to us in the weaknesses of the flesh, must not likewise the record of Him be clothed in the weaknesses of a book? This does not deny but insures the authoritative character of the Bible, because such is God's way of manifesting Himself in the world. An open heart and an open mind, seeking in faith God's truth for the world, will, as a result of keeping open, find the milk and the meat of the Gospels. Besides lengthy reading for information, small passages must be perused, preferably in succession, and thoroughly digested until they are assimilated at the subconscious background of thought. The spiritual life cannot be valid if we read the newspaper more leisurely and readily than the good news of God.

In the second place, one ought to find a few minutes each day to dwell with the great saints of the Church. Let me be frank in admitting that my own life suffers when I do not feed it on wise devotional reading as well as when I do not pray with some who know intimately the life of prayer. Those whose writings have helped me the most are Fénelon, De Sales, à Kempis and Oldham. Fénelon, that wondrously wise spiritual guide, can be read in two American translations, *Christian Perfection* and *Spiritual Letters*. De Sales' *The Devout Life* and à Kempis' *The Imitation of Christ* are well known. The book which I have used the most has been Oldham's *Devotional Diary*. For many years I have gone over and over it both by myself and with my classes. Baillie's *A Diary of Private Prayer*, Gore's *The Lord's Prayer*, Vernier's *Not as the World Giveth*, Clark's *I Will Lift Up Mine Eyes*, Heard's *Prayers and Meditations*, Bunyan's *Grace Abounding*, Munro's *Truth for Today*, Huegel's *Fairest Flower*, Boehme's *The Way to Christ*, Kierkegaard's *Edifying Discourses* and *Christian Discourses*, Phillips' *The Choice Is Always Ours*, Blakney's *Meister Eckhart* are titles taken almost at random which I have ingested slowly, savoring their wisdom day by day. When I fail to seek such nurture I feel a hunger and a weakness which I know are real.

Such reading need not consume much time, but it must be done slowly, steadily, and thoughtfully. To become practitioners of the spiritual life we must live with the masters and profit from them. One word of caution is necessary, not to indulge your own taste exclusively. Live day by day with both spiritual radicals and conservatives. Read Augustine, *The Prayer Book* (Episcopal), Fox, Wesley, and Woolman, and modern devotional writers of all creeds and persuasion.

I also feel the need of much more reading in non-Christian literature. How else can one learn to know these religions intimately unless we live with them slowly and as far as possible profoundly? I have been surprised at the depth and devotional character of the best in Bahai scriptures as presented, for instance, in Townshend's *The Promise of All Ages*. Can truth hurt us if we serve her with all our heart, or can its universal speech separate us from the love of God in Christ Jesus our Lord? Let us not repudiate any means of growth. But let us also hold fast our original and primary guides, pre-eminently the Bible.

The third kind of reading that should be done to strengthen the spiritual life might be called study. The mind must be well exercised if it is to be fit to serve the well-being of the whole person. The spirit needs the new light which the mind can bring it. Growth depends partly on hard study. For the development of the devotional life books like Whiston's *Teach Us to Pray,* Buttrick's *Prayer,* or Harkness' *Prayer and the Common Life* ought to be studied carefully for content. Undiluted theology also should be grappled with. Theology deals with problems which perplex the self and stunt its growth. Every person should seek out the theology that answers his questions as to the why of things, the problem of evil, the ways of providence, the nature and destiny of life. But study comes second, not first. First in order are worship and prayer. But real advance raises many questions for the intellect, though the process of growth also produces the answers to those questions. Thus we can learn from those who have faced these perplexities and found an answer that really satisfies.

Watch out for easy answers that are not as complex as the problems of life. They are short cuts and substitutes to avoid. The true answers are both as simple as the saint makes them and as complex as the world in which he lives. Watch out, too, for comforting answers that demand little of the asker. They are the theologies of the false prophets that have no real Gospel. The truth is as satisfying as the all-dependable and all-concerned love of God but also as hard as the Cross He offers the self both to die on and from which to derive new, wondrous life. Find the theology that answers your intellectual needs to see for yourself, that demands everything of you, and that leaves you still restless for the fuller truth and the better life. No other theology is good enough or true enough. Without real satisfaction of mind, however, there can be no genuine well-being for the soul. Without peace of mind there cannot be peace of soul.

You also need stimulus to keep going. Get yourself a partner with whom to discuss what you have read. Organize a study group to wrestle with the Bible or with theology. Get yourself a prayer partner too. Such a partnership may endure for years. Or it may last only for a number of months and then a new one may be formed. During the years I have had a number of people who have prayed with me more or less regularly and have helped me more than they were aware of. Do not, however, become dependent upon them. Learn to pray in the closet more and more, even while you cultivate the companionship of the two or three. You may never know how much you need someone else to share your experience before you have tried such sharing. The selection of a partner or partners must be more or less obvious and natural. Spiritual companionship cannot be forced. Open the door of your life and let God and others do the rest as far as the solution of this need goes.

You may find a prayer group which you may join. Lose

yourself in it. Often ministers are too self-conscious and are too much used to the prima donna role to get a group really going. That is the very reason, however, that they must succeed here, or know that they have failed to bear the fruits of faith. The new life will come largely through prayer. The new world will also come largely through prayer. It will come bit by bit as more and more learn to be genuine in their quiet and constant seeking to know God and to do His will. Thus housewives, farmers, railroad porters, businessmen find the occasion to sustain radiant prayer groups.

Never try to force group solidarity or complain about its failures. Examine, rather, your own life and provide more power for fellowship within your own prayers. Often I despair, for instance, about the possibility of real prayer among seminary faculties and students. Yet some of my holiest memories are from such bending before God in seminaries to share each other's problems and joys. Keep on believing and waiting and see if creativity does not blossom around you wherever you are. When people pray believingly things happen more than appears on the surface. However halting and sporadic, perhaps even occasional, be such a prayer group, thank God for it and take courage to use better whatever door is opened to you.

Certainly we have failed the churches at this point. The prayer meeting has generally died by default. Perhaps it had to die. Modern education, particularly the general interest in popular psychology, has dampened people's desire to reveal their inner selves. If anything, however, ought to help us to have better prayer meetings it should be the knowledge of psychology. We can now understand ourselves better and use this very psychology to test the spirits. The prayers and testimonies which center in the will of God and the common good have nothing to fear from psychology. The lives that long for nothing except to be rid of the drives which hurt the self and others need have no fear of being understood. They witness not to their own goodness but to the sufficiency of God's grace. We have grown afraid of one another, of strangers within the walls of the church, which walls divide the lives of us all. What we need is to be set free from these barriers.

Personally, I can think of no place I want to be known so well as on my knees confessing my own sins and faults and finding the strength and forgiveness to start again. I know no way to find fellowship so real and so lasting as within circles of prayer. We need more wisdom to conduct prayer meetings. Above all we need the spiritual fire to have them correspond to reality within the participants. Religion becomes a sham unless we ourselves are constrained by it, and we never shall be until we pray as individuals, families, groups, and churches.

All the prayer and study in the world, however, will never make God real or change our lives unless we live so that our "prayers be not hindered." As individuals and as families we must examine our lives in the light of the Gospel, submit to being judged by it, and be enabled by it to achieve lives full of healing and help. Over and over again we fail. Such is the way of all true growth in freedom. But through all failures of dedicated spirits runs a line of growing reality, transformed attitudes, and effective action. God never fails us if we trust Him for a new kind of life.

There are some definite rules, moreover, for real Christian living. First of all we must surrender our whole selves to God, both their conscious and the subconscious constituents. This takes time. A very prominent professor in one of our seminaries confessed that after four hours of trying to find full surrender, a few spiritual leaders became very much discouraged. They were still not much different in their feelings and thoughts. Total surrender takes at least a lifetime. When our present self finds surrender, moreover, God lets us have ever larger selves to surrender! Certainly Jesus had to keep surrendering to the end, through Gethsemane and Calvary. The saints know what years of self-offering are involved. As one area is won they have found that God lets us find another to be used for him. Spiritual pain and sense of failure must be no source of worry, for guilt feelings always accompany the growing life. When God declares present attainment inadequate His judgment makes us feel guilty about it; but how else could we ever keep growing? Be concerned, rather, if you feel that your life has attained its fulfillment. Especially be concerned if you suspect that you are a saint. Surrender is the hardest thing life offers and uses up all the time we have.

Surrender, however, is not negative but positive. We should, perhaps, instead of surrender, call it the constant acceptance of God's gracious will. Surrender, however, is the opening of the door which God will not break down. Surrender is our job. Our surrender is made to God who gives us freely all things. We surrender the narrow, shut-in self to find the wide-seeing and free self. We surrender the self that is feverishly and vainly set on its own way to find God's life-satisfying way. We surrender the self that nourishes its own hurts and prejudices to find the self of fellowship which rejoices in other people's joy and finds redemptive gladness in helping their hurts. Surrender is the door, the abundant life beyond it is the heart of the Christian faith.

Surrender becomes cheap and evasive, nevertheless, when it is merely or mostly an emotional formula for feeling secure with God. Real security does not come about that way, for God is no dispenser of comforts to pious prigs. Surrender to God means genuineness of life, first of all. It is self-acceptance. It is seeing oneself as one is, in need of being remade. It is no longer feeling sorry for the self but finding faith to remold that self for the common good. Always and ever the Christian life is tested by its fruits. Does the person become more outgoing and less self-involved, not in talk and sermon but in actual deeds? Does he become more thoughtful of others? Does he become more willing to accept blame and less willing to criticize? Does he become more disciplined and less self-indulgent? Does his horizon grow and do his concrete concerns expand from self and family, to neighbors and community, to the church and the Church Universal, to the nation and the world? Does he accept responsibility and do things, or does he find fault and make excuses?

Christianity is not worth the breath it takes to say the creed unless it can produce individuals who have found in concrete living a new community commitment in every dimension. A rabid sectarian, a racialist, a sectionalist, a nationalist shows by his fruits that his heart is full of something that is not Christianity. In Christ there is no overagainstness but a complete concern for all. Christ is the love incarnate that casts out fear. Most of our thinking is based on fear. It is defensive. We see criticism in what people say. We find bad news most interesting because we ourselves live in fear. We build theologies of fear in the name of the dispeller of fear.

As sure as Christ is Christ a real Christian breaks down barriers among groups at home, among the churches, in the communities, and to the ends of the earth. Unless a Christian has his whole life set on the making of effective peace, positive and creative, his is a vain confession. The Christian makes grace abound or he is no channel for the Christ. New attitudes and new actions are always involved in the genuine article which is the Christian faith.

Particularly important is the matter of giving. The Christian first of all gives his whole life and all that he is and has. He has to struggle to keep back what he is saving to provide for the future security of his family or for other responsibilities. The Christian rejoices in giving. Perhaps it is wise to set aside in prayer some such sum as 10 per cent of one's wages for Christian purposes.

I do not mean to devise any legalistic formula, but unless there is some regular way of giving, much energy is lost in deciding about each particular occasion. Find out what satisfies your heart in God's sight, and then give it joyously. One must not keep giving because of guilt feelings. Never grieve over giving what you have decided upon *before God* when you happen to be short of money, nor grieve because you have no more to give. God has ample physical means. What He needs is for you to give in faith and as a dedicated answer to His voice in your heart. Perhaps you may be counted on to give more during some particular occasion. During the war many young couples perhaps felt called upon to give more than seemed wise at the time, but in retrospect they see that everything worked out well. Certainly if you do not like to give you know well indeed where your heart is not.

The amount is not what counts the most, though we obviously must be careful not to delude ourselves on this score. What counts the most is what we give, how we give, and why we give. We all want to give to the church to bless it and make it a blessing. Let the church of God be ever well supplied. But ever as Christians let us give to good community and secular causes. Let us give where actual need is effectually met with as little overhead expense as possible.

We should give quietly and perhaps scatter our gifts rather widely so as not to become too important to any organization. Some causes we support regularly; others as the spirit moves us. There may be so many calls on our pocketbook that we cannot contribute to all. One saint I know answers every appeal, and he has many, even if with only a dollar. He gives and gives never despairing. Others have to say no and focus their response at least to some extent. No rule can be set except that we ought to give to organizations that cover the full gamut of spirit, mind, and body. Let the whole man be served. This means that some organizations will be definitely spiritual in their aid, others educational, and still others will render mostly physical services. Particularly important for Christians is, of course, to give wisely to unpopular causes, where fears and narrow pressures prevent most people from giving at all. Need I mention that our dependants near and dear are a primary obligation, as Jesus himself pointed out?

Giving should be both wise and dedicated. Preferably the whole family should participate in it. Children learn to give and to worship through giving. Children should know where the gifts go, and even how and why. If a certain sum represents the regular family giving, special love offerings should be made besides, at Thanksgiving and at Christmas, perhaps when God blesses the family unexpectedly, or when hearts feel particularly thankful. Perhaps a child will pray for someone to whom you used to send CARE packages. Let yourself be moved to match that prayer of concern with a new package *that very day* and let the whole family thank God for the privilege. Much giving has to be impersonal, but occasionally give something special like a goat to Japan or send packages to some saint abroad who is not exactly starving, but whom God wants to bless by being remembered. The wife may feel strongly about some cause of her own. Let her have money for her use. The husband may have his own reasons for some private giving. Let him do so in secret. Much blessing, growth, and joy is definitely lost because our lives are not genuine channels of love.

Above all, give in prayer and thanksgiving. Present the check at the family altar. Take the pledge card to the prayer circle. There is a difference between a cup of cold water and giving it in Christ's name. The difference is no superstition but hard fact. When we give in Christ's name we give gratefully to God and for the common good as privileged instruments. No sense of superiority is to be taken from Christian giving, only the joy of being counted unworthy servants. But unworthy servants may be accepted as actually friends and sons of God!

To strengthen the spiritual life we must use the "divine formula:" Worship, work, wait. We shall never improve personal or family devotions apart from these three means of strengthening the spiritual life. Only as we worship God can we work for Him to the fullest advantage, guided and constrained by His inclusive concern. Only as we work genuinely for the common good can we feel the need for the worship where the whole self cries for God to help us with our puny efforts to make His reality known and to make a better world. Only as we wait can we learn that growth does not depend upon us but upon Him who gives the increase, we know not how.

Pray we must, study we must, give we must; but above all we must find our lives bathed in the reality of God's faithfulness. As we worship, work, and wait, we shall become surprised that, as God becomes more and more real, we may come to feel ourselves less and less worthy and able. But others will find strength and help from us and tell how serenity and strength increasingly characterize our spiritual life. All of life's values will become steadily changed. Though we cannot ourselves understand why and how, the fever of life is over, and we experience a healing and well-being beyond our deserts.